Bahati and Beyond.

Part two of my Autobiography.   Ian G. McDonald

Introduction .

This book covers my 23 years as a fishing boat owner and trophy winning skipper in the Scottish fishing industry. It covers many amusing and tragic events that befell me and my crew during this period. I became deeply involved in fisheries politics and was a thorn in the side of governments of whatever party as they seemed hellbent on destroying our historic industry. I appeared many times in the national media fighting our corner. On one occasion I even found myself addressing a major committee of the EEC in Strasburg on one serious issue. I left the crumbling industry before I was forced out and started a new chapter of my life in the traditional Scottish Salmon Fishing industry. I spent 7 years operating a coastal salmon fishing company. Once more I became involved in the political fight to keep this industry in existence. We were faced with the greed of the river landowners and their lobby in the upper house who wanted all the salmon for themselves to add value to their estates and river fishing rights. These rights were held by the very same titles as our netsmen held theirs. If things were not so tragic for some it could have been a hilarious comedy.
Despite the seriousness of these situations I have tried to keep the book amusing as well as informative.

About the Author

Ian Gent McDonald was born on 15th February 1937 in Banff in North Scotland, moving to Stonehaven near Aberdeen in 1947. He was educated in Scotland at the Banff Academy and Robert Gordon College. Agriculture was his second choice of career but he enjoyed his time as an agricultural trainee in Scotland on the Tilquhilly estate in Deeside and at the University of Aberdeen Faculty of Agriculture. This equipped him for his post as Agricultural Field Officer in Tanganyika from 1958-1963, although he needed a crash course in coffee cultivation and Swahili language when first arriving there.

McDonald would have preferred to go to sea but later, satisfied this ambition by becoming firstly HM's Fisheries Field Officer on Lake Victoria (1960) and then responsible for Tanganyika's inland fisheries until 1961. After a long leave, he returned to Africa and, living in KIGOMA, the main port on the Tanganyika shore of Lake Tanganyika where he became responsible for the fishing industry on Lake Tanganyika until his return to the UK in 1963.

McDonald remained closely involved with the Sea Fishing Industry in Scotland until 1986, becoming a fishing boat owner and successful trophy winning skipper in addition becoming a director of the Scottish Fisherman's Federation and arguing for a fair deal for fishermen at the highest levels of government. Since the demise of a coastal salmon fishing venture – which failed because of legislative changes in 1991 – McDonald has made his living as a professional photographer, initially social and domestic but additionally as an internationally published glamour photographer. He closed the studio door when he retired in February 2002.

In 1958, he married Lilian Laurenson from the Shetland Isles. Lilian has been his stalwart companion and is the mother of his four children. Ian McDonald is a man who likes to speak his mind and Lilian is a strong, independent-minded woman. Even so, or perhaps because of this, they celebrated their Golden Wedding in August 2008.

BAHATI AND BEYOND.

Chapter 1.

On return from our years in Africa one of my first jobs was to go and see the White Fish Authority regional manager in Aberdeen. I went to meet with him to try and negotiate a loan under the government grant and loan scheme to enable me to build my first commercial fishing boat. I wanted to build a traditional 56 foot Scottish seine net fishing boat. With this in view I filled out all the necessary forms on the loan application and had to arrange to get competitive tenders from three independent boat building yards. Once this application had been safely lodged Lilian and I and our kids were able to set off up to Shetland to see the other set of grandparents. We only stayed in the Shetlands for about two weeks and then returned to Stonehaven to set about house hunting. Ideally I would have liked to find a house to rent relatively close to Stonehaven Harbour but in the event I had to settle for a cottage about 2 miles outside town. I was able to rent this cottage from a farmer that I had known in my dairying time in Stonehaven. Once the housing situation was sorted I was lucky enough to find a job as a deck hand on one of the local fishing boats. This at least I hoped would give us a living wage so as not to use up our meagre financial reserves, as we would need all the money we possessed to make the necessary deposit for the building of any boat. Several weeks later we received word from the whitefish authority headquarters in Edinburgh that our loan application had been refused. We were told that they were not intending to finance the building of any additional boats of that size in the immediate future. They said however that they were prepared to finance the building of a smaller class of boat providing that I could find a working partner in the boat, as it was not their policy to offer financial assistance to any single individual preferring partnerships in any venture. By chance an old school friend had just returned to Stonehaven with his family having recently completed his service in the Royal Navy as a clearance diver. When I propositioned him about the possibility of going fishing he jumped at the chance and so a new application proposal was prepared and submitted to the White Fish Authority for the building of a thirty six foot class of inshore boat. Once again competitive tenders had to be sought from three independent boat building yards and the tender that was selected came from John Watt and Sons of Banff. By chance this boatyard was situated only some 300 yards from where I had been born some 26years previously. Our joint deposit was paid to the boat builder and so the building of the vessel could commence.

At this time a very senior international marine scientist who I had known since my school days, came home to Stonehaven on holiday. He came to see me and offered me a position as his assistant in his post with FAO stationed in the Caribbean. This opportunity was very tempting and I was to receive an official application form from FAO headquarters in Rome to formally apply for this post. I started to fill in this application form which could be more closely described as a small book. I got to the section dealing with languages spoken and immediately thought to myself that if I filled in this section with Swahili and the fact that I had already assisted in the compilation of an FAO report from East Africa there would not be much chance of me being posted to the West Indies. Lilian and I sat down and had a serious discussion about our situation and came to the conclusion that as our deposit had already been paid for the building of the boat I had better decide to remain at home in Scotland as we would undoubtedly have to return here at some point in the future. I told Bill my scientist friend of our decision and let the offer slip from my mind. I had never even enquired as to what the likely remuneration for the post would be. But three weeks later the post was advertised in the International Fishing News and I was amazed to see that the starting basic salary was US$10,500 per annum. When you are employed by FAO you are not subject to local income tax and so this annual salary was multiples of anything I had ever dreamt of earning before. Too late, we had to live with our mistake as the boat was already beginning to take shape. This was just another example of the many mistakes I have made in my life.

In due course the boat was ready for launching, and our two families gathered at Banff Harbour for the event. The boat had been built on the quayside and as a result was going to be launched sideways into the harbour. Several large beams had been placed under the keel so that the boat would slide sideways gracefully down onto the soft sand at the bottom of the harbour. Once again things didn't go according to plan. The hull had just moved out beyond the edge of the pier when there was a loud cracking and splintering sound as one of the support beams broke under the weight and the boat hull fell the last three or 4 feet down onto the sand of the harbour floor. A thorough inspection was carried out, but it was found that no damage had been done to the hull. A wire was quickly attached and the boat was winched down into the water, the two young daughters of the partners breaking the champagne bottle on the stern of the boat rather than the stem and proudly naming the boat Bahati. We had decided upon this name from our time spent in Africa. Bahati is the Swahili word for luck but it is usually applied with the qualification of either good or bad. We didn't however dare to make that application.

During the next several months we made almost weekly visits to Banff to see how the fitting out work was progressing. When you are waiting a completion date like this it seems to take forever, but eventually the engine and winch were installed and all other work was completed and the date was set for sea trials and acceptance. The sea trials had to be conducted in the presence of the senior White Fish Authority marine surveyor who was there to carry out checks on all of the mechanical and safety installations. Once all his checks had been carried out to his satisfaction we could sign off our acceptance of the boat and were able to set sail for our home port of Stonehaven.

When we arrived at Stonehaven harbour we discovered that a second new boat had arrived in the harbour on the very same day. It seemed remarkable that two new boats should arrive in the town simultaneously when no other new vessels had arrived in Stonehaven for over thirty years. The other boat was called the Sweet Promise and was of a similar size to ours and she also had been built by a partnership of two local young men. There was plenty of interest shown by the local fishermen and towns folk in these new arrivals, but we were more concerned with getting our fishing gear on board and making everything ready for our first fishing trip. I am delighted to say that when we finally got to sea for the first time everything functioned perfectly and we started to make reasonable catches right from day one. Our initial success however didn't last for long. In the middle of the second week just as we came round the headland to approach the harbour our engine suddenly stopped leaving us drifting perilously close to the edge of the cliffs. Fortunately another local boat was following some hundred yards astern of us and I was able to contact him via radio and let him know of our situation. We made a rope ready to pass to him when he reached our position and he was able to tow us safely into the harbour. On examination we discovered that the crankshaft of the engine had broken which would mean that we would have to get an immediate engine replacement. The boatyard and engine manufacturers were contacted and a week later with our second engine installed we were ready once more to proceed to sea. We continued to fish out of Stonehaven for the remainder of that late summer and autumn regularly making catches in line with the other boats of our class.

I regret to say that my choice of engine had not been the best and we frequently lost costly sea time and incurred crippling expenses over the following years due to engine failures. A total of seven engines had been replaced before we saw sense and left our British manufacturer and installed a Swedish Volvo 120Hp engine that in the following years gave absolutely no trouble at all. This is yet another illustration of my costly mistakes in life. We continued to fish out of Stonehaven for the remainder of that late summer and autumn regularly making catches in line with the other boats of our class.

In early November we heard of a substantial sprat fishery that had developed up in the inner Moray Firth. This fishery was being carried out with the use of pair trawl. this method of fishing required the use of two boats pulling a midwater trawl net between them. If we wanted to go to this fishery we would have to find a partner. Another new boat of similar class to Bahati was almost complete at the Banff boat building yard so I went up to Banff to meet with the skipper of this boat, to see whether he would be interested in forming a partnership with us to exploit this new fishery. The boat was called the Misty Isle and was being built for a father and two sons, one of the sons being the skipper of the new boat. Having come to an agreement about forming a pair team I then had to purchase a pair trawl and make some minor modifications to the boat to be ready to exploit this type of fishery. Once delivery of our fishing partners' new boat had been accepted we set off to sail up to Inverness to meet our partner boat so that we could commence pair fishing for sprats and herring. The principal advantage of fishing in the sheltered waters of the inner Moray Firth in winter time meant that our small class of boat lost very little fishing time due to bad weather. A very large fleet of all classes of boats had gathered in the Firth to carry out this sprat fishery. The daily catch potential of the fleet exceeded the possible marketing capacity, so the fishermen had formed a committee who were responsible for allocating a daily quota to restrict the catch to balance with the daily potential market. At the height of the season more than 200 boats were involved in this fishery. The quota was allocated on the basis of a fixed number of crans per man in each crew. A cran is the traditional volume measurement used for landing herring and sprats. One cran equals four volume-certified baskets full of fish. This meant that big boats with as many as 10 men on board competed fairly with boats such as ours with only five men. There were so many boats and so much fish that at times the fleet had to be divided into two and you only got to fish on alternate days. If you succeeded in catching your full quota however you were guaranteed to make a reasonable living wage working in conditions that were far more favourable to our smaller class of boat than working on the open sea.

It was an unbelievably severe winter that year and even the brackish water in the sea firth at times froze. A couple of times while fishing at night the frost was so severe that while hauling up, the ropes would ice up completely in the time it took to travel from the stern rollers to the winch which was near the bow of the boat. While passing over the winch barrels and through the coiler splinters of ice where coming off the rope. The resultant coil of rope lying on the deck would then freeze together and the next time you paid it out as you shot the net, it made a sound like tearing sacking with ice splinters flying everywhere. Because we never expected to experience these sort of temperatures the bottled gas that we used on the boat to fuel our heater and cooking stove was the normal calor gas in grey cylinders. If we were tied up in the harbour overnight we discovered that the cylinders would freeze, and so first thing in the morning it became a routine for everyone to go on deck and piss onto the gas cylinder. This would release enough gas to boil a kettle of water which could be poured over the cylinder to give you enough gas to make the breakfast. Once the boat engine was started up and had gathered some heat you could keep the gas melted by turning the deck hose on to the cylinder from time to time. We quickly discovered that to overcome this problem we had to convert to using methane gas delivered in the red cylinders. This type of gas did not suffer from the same low temperature problem and made life aboard much easier.

The daily catch of the fleet was landed to a variety of outlets. There were two Norwegian freezer factory boats moored in the harbour that received their total processing capacity daily. There were also normally two or three cargo boats anchored out in the Beauly Firth. These boats acted as Klondikers, the fishing boats discharging their catch directly into them, where the fish were boxed and covered in ice to keep the cargo in good condition until it was transported to one of several European countries. Several large lorry loads of fish were also purchased daily by some of the main fish canners in Scotland, with the balance of the catch being transported to the fish meal factories for reduction into fish meal and fish oil. All these various outlets bought the fish at varying prices so the fishermen's quota allocation committee had to make suitable alternations to each quota to ensure that the fishermen involved would all receive a relatively similar wage. Bahati was only capable of carrying some 85 crans. With this amount of fish on board she was virtually awash and from any distance away all you could see were the masts and wheelhouse showing above the water. This gave rise to our nickname among some of the fleet as the little submarine. That particular year at Inverness this fishery continued right up until the end of February before the fish shoals retreated out into the open sea and brought our season to a close.

Financially it had been a very good season for us and set us up in a relatively sound financial situation so that we could meet our payments on the loan for the boat and have a margin left over to work with. Once we got back to Stonehaven we had to return to the seine net fishery for whitefish. This was a severe shock to the system after working for these months in the sheltered waters of the inner Moray Firth. Fishing in the inshore waters at this time of year was historically always very poor. Traditionally the month of March was referred to as the hungry month of March. This year was no different and we had a hard time trying to make ends meet until the beginning of June when more fish began to appear in the coastal waters. The fish that did appear tended to be rather small in size and although big enough to be legally landed they were only fetching a very poor price, frequently as low as 12 to 14 shillings per seven stone box. This meant that you had to land an awful lot of fish to make any money at all even then not showing any real profit. To try to improve the situation we started having to venture far greater distances out to sea. There we caught a better class of fish but the small size of the boat set a tight limit on the size of the catch that we could carry and keep in a well chilled condition until we reached market. This in turn meant that we had to spend more time sailing to and from the fishing grounds in order to land our catch in good condition. We had to land at least every second day while the bigger boats we were fishing alongside could continue fishing for the full four days and even more if it was required. Our small crew of only three men also meant that you had to endure long spells of very hard work with very little sleep and with only a very modest wage to show for all your efforts at the end of the week. I was frequently very concerned as to whether we were making enough money to keep up repayments on the purchase of the boat but somehow we always seem to manage to make it. We were frequently thinking back to the good times we had at Inverness at the sprat fishery and hoping that the sprats would once more return to the sheltered waters and let us catch our breath and make some money again.

In late October the skipper of our partner boat the Misty Isle telephoned me to say that there was once more the appearance of sprats coming into the Moray Firth. He was working out of Burghead fishing for prawns and was seeing shoals of sprats on his echo sounder and also seeing the gathering numbers of seabirds circling over the shoals. He was keen that we should sail up to Burghead to fish alongside him at the prawns until the sprat shoals reached a density that we could start fishing for them. We did not have and couldn't afford to buy a prawn net to go to this fishery for only a short time but he said he could lend us a net and trawl doors to keep us going. I agreed to his suggestion and so we once more made the boat ready for the sprat fishery and set off to sail up to Burghead. There we borrowed his spare trawl doors and prawn net and started in the new venture of fishing for prawns. It's normal practice in the Moray Firth to trawl for prawns during the hours of darkness as in the clear water in that area the prawns only come out of the mud to move around at night. We found that the prawn fishing was like a holiday compared to the work that we had been carrying out while seine netting for white fish. We had to spend comparatively little time at sea but required the use far less horsepower and therefore fuel than in our normal fishery. We were amazed at the end of the first week to find just how much more money was left for wages from what we thought was a minimum amount of effort. It certainly made us think about what we might do in future. Near the end of the second week at Burghead along with the Misty Isle we sailed up into the inner Moray Firth to have a look around with our fish finders to see whether there were indeed enough sprat shoals to allow us to start fishing for sprats. There were shoals but certainly not in the quantities of the previous year. The weather in the outer firth by this time was beginning to worsen resulting in lost nights at sea and lower catch rates. We jointly decided therefore that it would be worth taking the gamble and changed over our fishing gear to try fishing for sprats once more on the following week.

Little Bahati while buildind.

Bahati shortly after launching.

Bahati while fitting out in Banff Harbour.

Landing a good catch of sprats at Inverness

Bahati lost amongst the fleet at Inverness.

Fully loaded with sprats 84 crans in total.

Chapter 2.

We sailed from Burghead on the Monday morning and searched with our echo sounders for evidence of the sprat shoals as we sailed westwards up into the Firth. It was lunchtime before we started fishing but when we hauled we found that we had to release the catch because it was a mixture of sprats and small herring and you were not allowed to land a catch that contained a major by-catch of immature herring. We continued farther west and did manage to catch enough marketable sprats to make a small landing that night. We were back in business. The following day we ventured into the Beauly Firth and when we shot our gear we caught a big haul of clean Kessok herring, enough to fill both boats. Good marketable herring were of course far more valuable than sprats. We thought it must be Christmas and we would never be poor again. We were back at the quayside in Inverness by lunchtime landing our catch and dreaming of tomorrow and thinking of what our wage packet would be. It is quite amazing how quickly the news about catches of fish seems to travel. Our first day we had the whole firth entirely to ourselves. When we woke in the morning and looked down the river all we could see was a mass of fishing boat lights. The fleet had evidently arrived. There had been enough in the shoals of fish to keep our small boats satisfied but the number and size of the boats that had descended upon us during the night took only a few hours to sweep the firth bare of all fish. We decided by the Wednesday evening that there was not going to be enough fish to keep this fleet working. With our big haul of herring on the Tuesday we were already sure of a good week's wage, so we decided to go home early, leaving our boats in Inverness. We would return and see what the situation was on the Monday morning. The fleet that had gathered so quickly when news of our catch spread soon discovered just how few fish there were and departed for pastures new just as quickly as they had gathered. When we went out into the Firth on the Monday morning we found that there were only four or five pairs of relatively small boats similar to our own remaining in the area. The catches we made were by no means good but they were enough to sustain us and keep us working in these sheltered waters for several weeks. About a month later the shoals of sprats and herring gradually increased in number and density and the fleet gradually increased in number until quotas had once more to be enforced. We continued to be able to make a living fishing here until mid-January when suddenly the shoals of fish all disappeared. We were at a loss as to what to do because with this cold wild weather we knew that there would not be much opportunity for us making a reasonable wage while fishing out in the open sea.

We then came to hear that there was a good sprat fishing being experienced in the sea lochs of the outer Hebrides, with the catches being landed into Stornoway. We were also told that there were several pairs of smaller boats not much bigger than ours conducting this fishery. We held a meeting of our two crews and decided unanimously that we should go through the Caledonian Cannel to the West Coast and try our luck in this new fishery. As is usual at this time of year in the highlands it was bloody cold and we were informed that the canal was completely frozen along many of the inland stretches. You cannot sail an unprotected wooden boat along a canal that is frozen with unbroken ice up to an inch thick as it would simply cut the boat's hull into ribbons. We therefore had to clad our boats with big steel plates secured to and hung over the boat's rails reaching to below the water line, before we could entertain setting out on our voyage. The canal management fortunately keep these steel protective plates at the sea lochs where you enter the canal for use by any craft undertaking the passage in these icy conditions. Apart from the sea locks all the locks on the canal at that time still had to be operated by hand. This meant that the crew had to go ashore and screw open the sluices on the gates to allow the water to enter or leave each lock to equalize the level between locks. This proved to be quite hard and dangerous work because these sluice gates invariably were frozen to the lock gates and necessitated a high level of force and banging to get them to move. The planks that you had to walk on at the top of the gates to reach these sluice mechanisms were a solid sheet of ice making the task of reaching and winding the mechanism doubly hard and dangerous. Once the water level was equalized in the two locks you had to lay your backs against the big beams of the lock gates and gradually push them open to allow the boats to pass through. You then had to push these same heavy gates closed behind the boats and lower the sluices again before you could continue onwards, repeating the process time and time again as you proceeded along the canal. It was not too bad until we reached Fort Augustus at the west end of Loch Ness. At the staircase of locks there, the ice began to get really serious. Sometimes we were even having to push the ice flows with poles to make space in the locks for the boats to enter and progress. At the top of this staircase of locks the canal was just an unbroken sheet of ice as far as we could see. We were very apprehensive about trying to continue but "needs must when the devil drives" and so we made our way out into the canal. We managed to bump and barge our way along, often having difficulty in maintaining a true course as the ice sheets splintered and broke up as we forced our way ahead often pushing the boat's bow wildly to one side or the other as the ice broke up. Progress was very slow and we finally had to stop at the lock at the entrance to Loch Lochy when darkness fell. That is just about the highest point on the canal and I don't think I have ever felt as cold as it was that night. The cabin heater was not capable of keeping the cabin at a livable temperature and finally before midnight we resorted to starting the boat engine and leaving it running for the rest of the night. With the engine room door into the cabin left open we benefitted from the engine's heat. When we rose in the morning we discovered that the two boats had become completely frozen into the lock overnight. We thought we would be unable to move but fortunately when we lowered the water level in the lock the gradually tapered shape of the lock sides meant that the ice compressed and broke as we went down. A few minutes hard pushing with poles managed to move the resultant ice flows enough to allow us to escape out into the loch. You normally expect in a fishing boat that you can navigate the length of the canal in a single day, but this particular trip took us two full days to reach the Sea locks at Corpach at the west end of the canal. We were finally able to moor up there just after nightfall on the second day. There was a good covering of snow but it was not nearly as cold at sea level as it had been up in the hills on the previous night.

Captain Mc Donald the chief lock keeper on the canal came across to see us accompanied by his massive St Bernard dog. The pair were inseparable. He said that he would come down at around 5am when the incoming tide would have reached a level that would enable him to allow us to exit into the sea firth and continue on our way. He was as good as his word and promptly at five in the morning he was calling to us that the sea lock was ready and we could proceed in. Both boats started up. The Misty Isle was first to enter the sea lock and we followed close behind and secured our ropes to maintain position as the water level fell. As I said earlier only the sea locks at this time had been converted to hydraulic control and Capt. Mc Donald with his massive dog securely fastened to his left wrist was standing by the hydraulic control box. There had been a snowfall of about 5 inches during the night and he was completely enveloped in his big naval watch-keeping hooded duffel coat along with his heavy boots to ward off the cold. When ready he took his hands from his pockets and took hold of the controls to open the gates and let us leave the confines of the lock. The water level in the lock finally reached sea level and must have been at least 18 feet below the lock top surface. We could not see Capt. Mc Donald while we were in the lock and he could probably only see the top of our wheelhouses and masts. As soon as the gates were open wide enough the Misty Isle moved forward closely followed by our boat. In the meantime Jock, my partner in the boat and former Navy clearance diver, ran forward to the bow of our boat and tossed a very large ex-naval thunder flash onto the stern of the Misty Isle. Within seconds it detonated with a mighty explosion, the sound being magnified by the confined space of the sealock entrance. We could hear it echoing across to Fort William and up Loch Eil reverberating off into the distance. Suddenly we became aware of plaintiff howls and we looked in the direction of the sound just in time to see Capt. McDonald disappearing around the end of the buildings on the lock side being hauled at great speed on the end of his giant dog's leash, looking like a piece of cloth flapping in the wind in a Giles cartoon. There was certainly no way of stopping that dog once it got going, particularly if it set off with enough incentive. For years afterwards whenever Bahati passed through the canal Captain McDonald would always appear in an apparent foul mood looking for "that bastard with the beard".

We sailed away from the canal entrance at Corpach and set a course for the Corran narrows and onwards down Loch Linnhe making for the entrance of the sound of Mull. It was a beautiful morning and we made good progress sailing up the sound of Mull with a. strong tide behind us. We passed the entrance to Tobermory Bay and on out into the Minch round Ardnamurachan Point and then swung northwards to make a course to sail past the busy fishing port of Mallaig and onwards up the sound of Sleat making a passage between the island of Skye and the mainland. It had been a glorious day's sailing over glassy calm seas with absolutely no wind, and blue skies. As the whole passage had been relatively close to land we were still feeling the effects of the severe frosts onshore. This was in the days long before the Skye Bridge and we sailed through the narrows at Portree where the ferries plied back and forth from Skye to the mainland. We then altered course to sail up the inner sound and then onwards to pass to the north side of the Shiant Islands that lie between the north end of Skye and the Outer Hebrides taking us ever nearer to our goal of the sea lochs of the Outer Hebrides. We had heard plenty of chatter on our radios but had not been able to gather any information as to the state of the fishing, because all the conversation was being conducted in Gaelic. We sailed slowly northwards along the coast hoping to fall in with the fleet of boats that were sprat fishing but found no evidence of any activity. We were surprised by this lack of any obvious fishing effort as the reports we had received before we set off from Inverness led us to believe that the fishery was ongoing around-the-clock. When it was fully daylight we started exploring up into the confines of the sea lochs but failed to find any evidence of shoals of sprats or herring then just as it was getting dark we came upon some very good traces on the echo sounder and we decided to shoot our.net and tow seawards down the loch. We were progressing steadily along the loch and the sea birds were steadily gathering and diving over where our net would be, a strong indication that we were catching fish. Then suddenly both boats gave a shudder and then went ahead and then came to a stop and we realized our net had come fast on the seabed. The birds were going crazy and we could see the surface of the water turning white with escaped fish as we watched. Obviously we had had a good haul but all was now lost with a shattered net still fast on the seabed. We hauled back slowly on both boats and then three of the crew of the Misty Isle jumped aboard our boat to help in trying to haul the net aboard. We eventually managed to get the remnants of the net onboard but there was no catch and a large section of the lower half of the net had been left adhering to the seabed. We set off with our tails between our legs on course for Stornoway Harbour to haul our severely damaged net ashore to enable us to repair it. There was snow and slush on the quayside at the harbour and we laboured there for two days in miserable cold conditions before we were able to complete repairing the net. Even more frustrating was the fact that we discovered that the sprat shoals had disappeared on the day that we had arrived on Hebrides coast and there had been no catches made on the two days we had spent repairing our net. The skipper of the Misty Isle had spent 11 years working on a boat fishing out of Loch Clash as it was known in those days, nowadays better known as Kinlochbervie. He suggested that there were some sheltered lochs along that coast that we could try to search for any fish shoals. We set off from Stornoway on a calm frosty night at about 3am and made off across the Minch in the direction of Loch Clash. We listened for the early morning shipping forecast and were horrified to hear that a very deep depression was approaching and that we would soon be experiencing storm force winds coming in from the Atlantic. We therefore decided to change course toward Loch Broom as we thought that it was probably the safest anchorage to be in to have any shelter from the coming storm. We had just reached the outer entrance of Loch Broom when the wind started to pick up and by the time we had sailed on past the Summer Isles the wind was already reaching gale force. We were very glad to round the headland at Ullapool and sail up along the sheltering land towards the harbour. The harbour at Ullapool at that time was a very simple piled pier with a cross pier on its end. We found that the harbour was completely occupied by larger boats and so all we could do was to anchor in the most sheltered corner of the bay as close to the shore as possible. The wind by this time was absolutely screaming and it was very difficult to move about on deck without hanging on. We laid our anchor and thirty fathoms of chain in relatively shallow water. This should have been able to hold us at anchor without any problem, but the wind force was so extreme that the anchor chain instead of running along the seabed to the anchor appeared to be leading straight to the anchor and dragging it like a plough across the seabed. We had to haul all the chain back aboard and sail back in close to shore to relay the anchor. But this time we attached our three hundredweight pair trawl fishing weight about midway along the anchor chain in an attempt to keep better contact with the seabed. This modification made an immediate huge improvement but we still found that we were gradually dragging our anchor. We found that if we left the engine running in gear in the ahead position we could maintain our position without dragging the anchor any farther away from the shore. For two whole days we had to lie there with someone constantly on watch to ensure that we did not move out of position, shining our search light onto the shoreline every half hour or so during the night. In my 23 years as a skipper at sea this is the only time that I have heard the shipping forecast repeatedly advising us that we were to have up to force twelve or hurricane force winds in the coming hours. By the end of these two days the crews on both our boats were thoroughly fed up with the West Coast and everything about it. It became our urgent desire to return to the waters we knew on the East Coast as soon as would be possible. The wind finally fell away on the evening of the third night and the shipping forecast at midnight told us that we were to have lighter winds for the next 24 hours. At daylight we raised out anchors and set off down Loch Broom towards the open Minch. We did not however even reach Priest Island at the entrance to loch Broom before we decided to turn round and head back to Ullapool as the seas left over from the days of severe gales were absolutely mountainous and not for risking in our small boats. We took the opportunity to refuel our boats from a fuel tanker on the pier and this would ensure that we had enough fuel on board to reach home. The lunch time shipping forecast warned us that the calm weather was not going to last and that increasing winds were to build up during the coming night. We decided to go and have another look to see if sea conditions had improved during the 12 hours of calmer weather. Things did look much better and we made our way out to Priest Island and onwards out into the Minch. The swells however were still very high. We had to continue dodging out in a north westerly direction until we were several miles offshore before conditions would allow us to turn south towards the inner sound between Skye and the mainland while keeping these huge following seas on our quarter. We made rapid progress once we had changed course as each swell picked us up and pushed us forward like a surf board. Darkness soon fell and I suppose exciting would be one way of describing the roller coaster ride we experienced. When you looked astern out off the wheelhouse window you just saw the hill of water rushing down toward you in the glow of the stern light. Then you felt the boat rise underneath you as the wave passed under you. The wave obviously lifted the stern of the boat first leaving the bow of the boat hanging down over the slope of the wave, then with a roar the boat would gather speed as you surfed along on the forward slope of the powerful wave before it finally passed leaving you to await the next swell. There is relatively little habitation on the West Coast and we only had occasional glimpses of any shore lights as we sailed on through the night. As we passed Rue Rea lighthouse it brought home to us just how high the swells we were sailing in were as we only caught glimpses of the lighthouse as we reached the crest of each wave. We had no radar at this time in our small boats and were dependent entirely on the mark 12 Decca Navigator to keep a continuous track of our position as we sailed on. Our course altered to become more south-easterly and gradually we felt the swells reducing as we got a degree of shelter from the Scottish mainland. By the time we reached the narrows between Kyle and Portree we were at last in calm water but by then it had started to snow. The snow increased to become a whiteout blizzard as we were about to enter the Sound of Sleat. This sound is a relatively narrow passage with a treacherous tidal current. The Decca Navigator was never very reliable in these confined West Coast waters because of the radio-wave-diverting capacity of the close by mineral rich mountains. The blizzard conditions was the final nail in the coffin of the navigator and the needles on the three dials that should have been telling us our position were simply waving backwards and forwards and round and round and providing absolutely no information. We were now completely dependent on our echo sounder and magnetic compass to make a safe passage down this narrow sound. My companion skipper on the Misty Isle suggested on the radio that it might be better if I led the way because he said our forward mast headlight was much brighter than his. I can only presume he was joking because there was no way you could see more than 15 yards ahead of the boat however much light you had. I slowed the boat down because the tide was with us and I reasoned that if I let the tide drive us it would keep us in the channel and away from the shoreline rocks. At the same time I kept an eye on the echo sounder to make sure that we weren't getting into shallow water. Thankfully we emerged from the snowstorm into a beautiful clear calm night and could see the streetlights of Mallaig twinkling on our port bow and the lighthouse at Ardnamurachan flashing a welcoming guide in the distance. From this point on we had an uneventful return journey to the sealock at Corpach and into the Caledonian Canal for our return journey across Scotland and back to the less frightening North Sea on the East Coast. This was to be the last pair fishing season we had with the Misty Isle because once they had gone home to Buckie they removed their ropes and seine net winch and installed a new trawl winch with wire trawl warps so there was no possibility of us fishing as a pair team as long as we were still using ropes.

Bahati with a good haul of whitings off Shetland.

Bahati with Misty Isle waiting to land sprats on Klondyker.

Bahati alongside my brothers much bigger boat.

Bahati in her Gray paint after 10 years at Burghead.

Our partner boat the Misty Isle.

Some of the sprat fishing fleet at Inverness.

Chapter 3.

When we returned to Stonehaven it was still "the hungry month of March" and we decided that rather than go to sea we would give the boat a thorough scrub down and paint in preparation for the long hard summer ahead. We fished locally for a couple of months going offshore when the weather allowed, but we were still finding it very hard to make a decent living. I was speaking to a Shetland skipper in our fish salesman's office in Aberdeen one day, and he told me that the small boats in Lerwick in the Shetland Islands were all making a good living only going to sea for a few hours each night and working very close to shore only over half an hour from the harbour. This sounded too good to be true but as Lilian comes from the Shetland Islands and at that time was taking our children up there for a few weeks each summer for a holiday with their grand parents, it became an increasingly tempting proposition. My crew were quite happy to give it a try so without more ado we fuelled up and set off for the 24-hour voyage to Lerwick. The Shetland skipper I had chatted to in Aberdeen had given me the names of some of the local skippers and he told me that he would ask them to give me every help once I got up there.

I could not believe just how helpful these men proved to be, instead of telling me where to go and what to do as would be the best one could hope for anywhere else in Scotland. I found that to begin with they would physically come alongside with their boat and jump aboard us and take the helm and shoot our gear for us pointing out the vital local landmarks as they went along. I would never encounter this degree of assistance from fellow fishermen in any other area of the British Isles that we would find ourselves fishing in during my 23 years as a skipper. We spent the rest of the summer fishing these waters. My crew just could not believe how easy life was compared to the work that we had to undertake to make a living at home. At the height of summer in the Shetland Islands there is no real darkness, and it appears that the fish in these coastal waters would only go down to the bottom when the light level fell. None of the boats would start shooting their gear until the nearby lighthouse started to flash and this was referred to "as the time a night". Then as if this were a starting pistol all the boats would frantically start laying their gear and would continue shooting and hauling as fast as possible until the daylight was fully in at dawn. Then everyone set sail for the harbour at Lerwick to land the night's catch. We could not keep up the catch levels that the locals were making but we did manage to make it financially more worthwhile than trying to make a living at home. By the end of August this inshore fishery was coming to an end and so we followed the local boats round to the west coast grounds and fished out of Scalloway. Once more we were in the Atlantic here and weather conditions started to be a problem for a boat of our size. We soon realized that shortly we would have to return south to our home waters.

One of my wife's cousins was getting married and so the whole crew were invited to go along for the wedding. None of us had ever experienced a Shetland wedding before. It was to take place in the local village hall because that was the only venue that could accommodate the large number of people that were to attend. The ceremony itself took place in the local Parish Church in the afternoon then everyone trouped over to the village hall for the reception. After the meal and speeches the dancing started and continued throughout the night with frequent breaks for more food while all drinks were free and were constantly available. My crew and I had a great time and just could not believe the level of the hospitality shown to us relative strangers. When we could not keep going any longer we set off back to the boat at seven o'clock in the morning. We went back to sea the following morning still in a rather delicate physical state. We had the good fortune to catch a big haul of large whiting on our first haul of the day, as much fish as our boat could carry. We had to make for the harbour and spent the rest of the day gutting, washing and stowing our catch. We said our farewells and expressed our thanks to the locals prior to setting off with our cargo of one hundred and fifteen boxes of iced fish for the market in Aberdeen twenty-four hours sail away. Once again I'm afraid to say we paid the penalty for the small size of our boat, because the catch was not in the best condition when displayed on the market and we did not make as much money as we could have done.

We continued to fish in local waters until early November when hopefully the sprat fishing season would be coming around again. We had teamed up with another local small boat that like us was still using ropes to operate our pair trawls. Unfortunately when we reached the waters of the inner Moray Firth we found that there were not the usual large shoals of fish we had hoped for and only another two or three pairs of boats were trying to follow the fishery. We had to search widely over the entire area of the Cromarty, Beauly and Inverness Firths to make any viable catches often leaving the boats at Inverness and going home on a Wednesday night to allow the sparse fish shoals to gather again by the following Monday. If we managed to make three decent landings per week we were still far better off than trying to fish for whitefish in the open sea. We continued fishing these waters up until the Christmas break but there was disharmony amongst the crew on our partner boat and as a result they wanted to go home. We came to an amicable agreement and while they sailed home we left our boat in Inverness at the entrance to the Caledonian Canal with the intention of sailing to Cambeltown in the Firth of Clyde to allow us to fish out the winter in the more sheltered waters in that area. We hired a lorry to transport our whitefish gear up from home and then it returned south with our pair trawl gear to our store in Stonehaven. Cambeltown had been a harbour that historically some of our local boats had fished out of over the years, seeking to work through the worst of the winter months in more sheltered waters. In the past they had usually sailed to the West Coast through the Forth- Clyde Canal. That was a much shorter journey but regretfully that canal was now closed, leaving the Caledonian Canal as the only option now available to make this passage.

We returned north after the Christmas- New Year break and set off on our journey across Scotland. The weather at this time was wet and windy so we didn't have any ice to delay or impede our progress. The wind was coming from the southwest and was pretty strong making our passage along Loch Ness very uncomfortable and more than an hour longer than usual with the wind gathering strength all the time. By the time we had reached the head of the bank of locks at Fort Augustus the wind had risen to a severe gale and even the surface waters in the canal were being lifted and blown about like smoke. Despite being blown about by the wind and steering a rather erratic course we successfully negotiated the miles of canal until we entered the last canal lock before entering Loch Lochy. Here the lock keeper was very much against us proceeding out into the open loch because the wind was so strong. It took a deal of persuasion before he was prepared to open the gates and allow us passage emphasizing that it was at our own risk. We left the shelter of the lock and made our way down the narrow neck of the loch head into open water. We very quickly realized our mistake. We should have heeded the lock keeper. The almost hurricane force wind being funnelled down the narrow valley between the mountains was raising fairly considerable waves at this end of the 8 mile loch. These freshwater waves while not nearly as high were very much steeper and more closely spaced than those we were used to in the open sea. The result was that the our thirty six foot boat was almost standing on end every time we passed over a wave. If I tried to increase speed the boat didn't go over the wave but tried to go through it like a surfaced submarine filling the decks with water that didn't have enough time to clear before the next wave was upon us. If I slowed down too much we stopped making any headway and if I had tried to turn around it would have meant going broadside for a time with the possibility of capsize. Our only choice therefore was to try and carry on. Keeping my hand constantly on the throttle we managed to dodge slowly ahead gradually making headway despite going up and down like a demented hobbyhorse. Our living cabin in the boat was at the stern designed to be the most comfortable part of the boat when at sea. The oven door of our gas cooker was hinged so that it opened downwards. The movement in the cabin was now so severe that this door was banging open and shut on impact with every wave. We had to tie it shut by securing it to the guardrail round the cooker top. The main Inverness to Fort William road runs a short distance up on the hillside along the full length of this Loch. In wintertime in those years you never expected to see a lot of traffic on the road but this afternoon we noticed that there seemed to be a hell of a lot of vehicles parked along the road with people out of their vehicles looking down from the roadside. We then realized that we were providing the floorshow and entertainment and I must say that it would probably have looked quite exciting. After we had passed the half way point along the loch conditions did gradually improve and we were able to increase speed but it still took us 3 1/2 hours to navigate the Loch and reach the comfort of the first canal lock, a passage that would normally take just over an hour. We could go no farther that night as darkness was upon us but next morning dawned with a complete calm and blue skies and we were able to continue to the sea lock at Copach without any further incident. The tide was too low to allow us to exit the sea lock when we arrived there, so we decided to wait until high tide in the early morning before continuing our journey. The speed of the ebbing tide would then be helping us on our way. It was like a beautiful early spring day with clear skies when we set off in the morning and with the strong following tide we made a rapid passage down Loch Linnhe and virtually raced through the narrows at Corran with probably a six or seven knot tide helping us on our way. Things were very soon to change however. Very quickly the skies darkened over the mountains to the west and in no time at all we had a screaming gale descending on us from the mountains accompanied by a lashing horizontal rain. We edged our way towards the western shore of the sea loch to seek as much shelter as possible but even as close to the shore as we dared go conditions were not too comfortable. We had been intending to reach Oban that night but now in these conditions that was out of the question so we continued our slow passage along the western shore but conditions were getting no better and the weather forecast at lunchtime advised us that these gales were to continue for at least the next 12 hours. Just after we heard the shipping forecast we reached the entrance of a relatively small bay called Loch Choire. I decided that this was probably the best place to seek shelter until we could continue to Oban .We entered this small loch sailing on until we reached the most sheltered western end, here we laid two anchors with our thirty fathoms of anchor chain making a very secure mooring. We had experienced first hand at Ullapool in a previous year just how wild these West Coast gales could become. The gale continued to scream throughout the night and periodically I would get up and play the searchlight on the shore line just to make sure we hadn't moved. Then just as quickly as the storm had started things went quiet just before daylight and the wind fell calm. It's really quite amazing just how quickly the weather can change beside these high Highland Mountains. Having eaten breakfast we hauled the anchors aboard and set sail for

Oban, sailing south until we reached the end of Lismore Island and then altering course for the north entrance of Oban harbour. We made our way to the quayside and tied up whilst our cook went off into the town to get some bread and milk and other supplies. He had only been gone for a few minutes when the harbourmaster came down and informed us that we would have to get going as there had just been a severe storm warning issued, and there was absolutely no shelter for us against the piers at Oban. He told us that we should go across the bay and go as close as we could to the back of Kerrera Island and try to anchor there in the most sheltered spot we could find. Once the cook had arrived back aboard with our supplies we cast off and headed off across the bay. As we approached Kerrera we found that there already were several larger fishing boats anchored close to the shore, as we sailed passed one of the local boats the skipper gave me a shout and we went alongside his boat. He said that he was concerned that we were rather too small a craft to be trying to anchor off the island to weather the coming storm. He pointed out what appeared to be a stone built wall along the edge of the island but he told me that if I sailed to the northern end of this wall we could go behind it and up onto what had been a seaplane slipway during the war where he reckoned for our size of boat that was by far the best option we had. I thanked him for his advice and as it had just passed high tide we approached the wall and rounded the end of it and moored up on the inside of the wall. We were certainly as safe as houses in here and spent about six hours out of every 12 resting on the concrete floor of the slipway as the tide ranged in and out. A couple of hours later when the storm really broke we were very glad to have found such a secure mooring. We spent two days here listening to the screaming gale, occasionally in the daylight hours daring to look over the wall towards Oban watching the waves crashing onto the sea front and up onto the street. The shipping forecast on the evening of the second day informed us that the storm would ease during the night and that there would then be a 24-hour lull before another extreme weather system arrived. As promised it dawned fair and after breakfast as soon as we floated on the incoming tide we set off from our sheltered haven and made our way down Kerrera Sound and out into the still heavy swell running in the open firth. We rocked and rolled our way southwards until we rounded the point at the entrance to Luing Sound where we altered course more south-easterly and ran down the sound with the swell behind us as we made for the sea lock at Crinnan at the west end of the Crinnan canal. The Crinnan canal would then enable us to cross the north neck of the Mull of Kintyre in about four hours reaching the eastern end of the canal at Ardrishaig where we could exit the canal out into Loch Fyne and the firth of Clyde. Once out of the canal we sailed down Loch Fyne and then turning in a more southerly direction we voyaged on down and Kilbrannan Sound between the island of Arran and the Argyle mainland passing the little fishing harbour of Caradale until finally reaching the entrance to Cambeltown Loch and onto our journey's end in the harbour. Due to the extreme weather conditions we had experienced it had taken us more than a week to complete a voyage that we would normally expect to make in about 2 1/2 days. We began to feel that there must be something of a jinx about Bahati venturing to fish on the west coast as each time we tried to go there we encounter unbelievably bad weather.

Before setting out for Cambeltown I had got copies of fishing charts for some of this area from a skipper friend on the East Coast who had in past years fished these waters. We had enough information from these charts to enable us to start fishing right away, but the main area they covered was where the bigger boats worked off the south end of the island of Arran down towards Ailsa Craig. These were pretty exposed waters for small boats like ours unless weather conditions were really favourable. At that time fishing boats under 40 feet in length were allowed to seine net in any area of the Firth of Clyde and the large sea lochs opening into the Firth. This enabled us to fish in the far more sheltered waters encountered in these areas. The only trouble was that I did not have any information about these fishing grounds and the location of any wrecks or other obstructions that they may contain. However we quickly gained the confidence and became friends with some of the local skippers and they willingly passed on their knowledge of the main hazards of the local waters. There were only two or three of the local boats of our class that were in fact seine netting. The majority of the boats were using ropes, but the ropes were attached to trawl doors which were towed like a normal trawler to catch prawns as well as fish. This method of fishing was of course illegal but as with most of the west coast at that time that was only to be considered by the locals as an inconvenience not an obstruction. The boats involved in this type of fishing still carried all their seine net ropes on deck so that to the casual observer they were going to sea to use that legal method of fishing. The firth as with the rest of the West Coast was regularly patrolled and policed by fishery protection boats but these patrols failed to produce much of a stir as all the skippers received plenty of advanced warming over their radios and were fully aware of the protection vessels movements from the moment that it left its moorings until it was in visual contact. I was absolutely amazed how nonchalant and brazen some of these skippers could be, even with the close proximity of the protection craft. On one occasion I witnessed the protection vessel moving up fairly close to a fishing boat and calling to the skipper of the fishing boat by radio enquiring how long it was going to be before he would haul his net up so that his crew could inspect the gear. The fishing boat skipper responded that they had only just shot their gear and provided they didn't come fast the net should be up in about an hour's time. In the meantime, to the casual observer the winch on the fishing boat was going round and round and the ropes from the coiler appeared to be piling up on the deck just as if the boat was in fact slowly hauling in the ropes. In actual fact the clutches were not engaged on the coiler which allowed the winch to run but it was not recovering any rope. A coil of rope was in fact lying underneath the coiler on the deck and every six or seven minutes one of the deckhands would pick it up and drag it aft just as you would do if you were genuinely seine netting. Only, now the deck hand would place a foot in the middle of the coil of rope he had just taken aft and as he went forward up the deck he would slide this coil forward with his foot until it was once more under the coiler ready for him to pick it up again and drag it aft. The fisheries patrol boat observed that the boat did appear to be seine netting and it sailed off to inspect some other craft. I could not believe the cavalier attitude of the skipper but when I spoke to him later he said that you never took any avoiding action until you saw the whites of the eyes of the boarding party, at which point you slewed the boat violently and cut the ropes claiming that you had just come fast and your gear had broken away and you now had to attach a large grappling iron to the end of your ropes and set about towing this along the sea bed trying to the recover the lost net.

I also witnessed a variation of this procedure while fishing in the deep water off the northwest tip of Arran. . One of the local boats was towing up and down in the deepest of the water and had been catching quite good quantities of hake. This being a high value fish he didn't want to stop fishing despite the fact that the fishery cruiser was tied up to the pier at Loch Ranza less than three miles away. The officers on the fishery cruiser had obviously been observing his movements on their radar and the first thing the skipper knew was when one of his deckhands shouted that the rigid inflatable from the fishery cruiser was speeding full speed towards them. The skipper immediately stopped the boat and cut his ropes tying both ends together before dropping them over the side and of course taking bearings where he had left his gear. In the few moments it took for the fishery cruiser's small boat to reach them, he had secured a grappling hook and a chain to the end of a coil of rope and shot it away and was moving slowly forwards with a deck hand leaning on the rope to detect any contact between the grappling hook and the lost gear. The Cruiser's small boat came alongside and two of the men came on board inquiring what was going on. The skipper informed them that much earlier in the morning, they had just made the ends of the ropes secure to the winch and were starting to haul when the winch malfunctioned and they had lost both tails of their rope over the side. He explained to the officers from the fisheries boat that that was why he had been going up and down this particular stretch of ground for several hours but as yet he had not been fortunate enough to grapple their lost net or ropes. This information was relayed to the captain of the fisheries protection boat by radio and he then told the boarding party that one man should remain aboard the fishing boat to keep track of what was going on while the others were to return to the ship. After an hour or so the fishing boat skipper suggested to the crew man from the protection boat that he and his crew were all getting very tired and would he take the wheel for a turn so that they could go below and have something to eat. The crew man from the cruiser was quite happy to be of assistance and so the skipper pointed out to him the landmarks that he would need to maintain while continuing search for the lost gear and then he went below, leaving instructions that the man should just call out if he felt the rope going tight. Two hours later the fishery cruiser left the pier and sailed towards the fishing boat dispatching his small boat to pick up his crewman. Seeing the approaching boat the crewman began shouting lustily but to no avail. He then left the wheel and went forward down into the cabin to see what was going on to find all the fishing boats crew were in their beds and fast asleep. He roused them and the skipper was very apologetic explaining that they were just totally exhausted and thanking him for his assistance. By the time that the cruiser's small boat was alongside, the fishing boat's crew were all back on duty and made a point of thanking their guest from the fishery cruiser for his assistance. The chain and grapple had been attached to the end of only one coil of rope and with the depth of water that they had under them there was not a snowball's chance in hell that they could have grappled up anything. By the time that the cruiser was little more than a mile and a half away they had paid out more rope and got a hold of the missing gear and within the hour they were fishing again.

Chapter 4.

If the sprat fishery failed or was very poor over the ensuing years we became regular visitors to Cambeltown and the firth of Clyde. We never made a fortune while fishing in these waters but the shelter afforded in this location did enable us to make a reasonable living at a difficult time of year. We made the odd very good catch but the prices one achieved in remote Cambeltown, over a hundred miles from the Glasgow market, were never that good. On one occasion we had a haul of over 100 boxes of large Coley in the deep water right at the entrance to Cambeltown loch. We went right ashore with this haul in the best of condition but Robert McPherson the local fish salesman was unable to find a buyer locally so he consigned them to the market at Hull along with some other fish to make up a full lorry load. At the end of that week when they made up our sales sheet we discovered that we had in fact lost money on the consignment, the transport cost to Hull being greater than the price achieved for the fish. A small ticket attached to the settling sheet saying "please note no commission was charged on the sale" which I must say was of very small comfort. On another occasion in good weather we were fishing for cod at the Brown Heads off the south end of Arran along with several much larger boats from the Moray Firth. We were lucky enough to strike a haul of large cod and got it all on board as quickly as we could to get the gear set back in the same place with the hope of achieving a second similar haul. We had just taken the second end of our ropes aboard and had started towing when one of the much larger boats sailed close alongside as he was shooting out his set of gear. We heard the skipper announce over the radio that little Bahati was almost sunk with the weight of the quantity of cod aboard. He went on to describe how all our decks were absolutely awash with fish. Soon it appeared that all the big boats in the area were making for the patch we had been working. Although we got another good haul when we hauled up our net,we could not have found a gap amongst the big boats big enough for us to shoot in again. As it was we did not need to shoot again as our two hauls had caught as much fish as we could handle. On this occasion we didn't make for Cambeltown but instead set off over the firth to sail three hours east to land at the much larger fish market in Ayr. We caused no little consternation amongst the locals there to see such a small boat coming into the harbour to land so much fish. This I regret to say was one of our few really successful days' work. I'm afraid it was more normal just to be able to catch enough fish to keep our heads above water and make a moderate living for the crew. But at least in these relatively sheltered waters it did give small boats like Bahati a sporting chance of making a living during the wildest months of the winter.

We used to travel up and down from Cambeltown to Stonehaven in our car almost every weekend and sometimes we became caught up in some treacherous conditions often experiencing blowing snow, ice and high winds while on other occasions there would be lashing rain and floods. The worst conditions we ever encountered was going back to Cambeltown late on a Sunday night when a very severe gale struck Scotland lifting the roofs off many houses in Glasgow and Clydeside and flattening large areas of woodland right across Scotland. The conditions on the road that night where really quite frightening. The blasts of wind buffeting the car made it feel more like buffeting waves in the boat. We had to stop and haul broken branches off the road several times but just before we reached Loch Earnhead we were suddenly confronted by a wall of fallen trees across the road and so could obviously go no further. When we came to a halt we could hear that trees were still falling all around us and I got really alarmed. By pure chance about 5 yards behind us we spotted a farm gate opening into a grass field. I reversed back and drove the car off the road through the gate and out into the middle of the field where we felt relatively safe as we were well beyond the range of any falling trees. We had to remain there until after lunch time the next day when finally the road gangs with their chainsaws reached our location clearing the roads. When we finally got back on the road and made it through to Tarbert and then onto West Loch Tarbert we were amazed to discover two large 60 foot fishing boats washed up into the middle of a field two fields distant from the shore of the anchorage where they had been moored at West Loch Tarbert. Loch Tarbart opens into the Atlantic on the west coast of Argyll and the hurricane had been blowing right up the sea loch driving the water before it forcing it higher and higher as the loch narrowed resulting in the boats being dragged from their moorings and deposited up in the fields beyond. As we drove on we were just as surprised to find the fences at the roadside some considerable distance from the sea absolutely festooned with seaweed showing just how high the tidal surge had been.

We frequently used to encounter large numbers of deer on these remote west Argyle roads and they could prove to be quite dangerous if you encountered them lying on the roadway just as you came hurtling round a bend. These encounters provided more than a few exciting moments over the years. We were nearly always travelling in the middle of the night and on many occasions were stopped by the police patrols out on these lonely roads looking for deer poachers. It was a bloody good job that in those days the police were not equipped with speed cameras but on several occasions they made comments about our speed and safety. I had always been known as a bit of a speed nut, a fact that I am not necessarily proud of. Normally I just want to get from A to B in the quickest possible time and we regularly completed the 252 miles between Cambeltown and Stonehaven in between four hours 15 minutes and four hours 20 minutes. When this became known by the Clyde fishermen it gave rise to our unusual call sign when it sea. Everywhere else that we have fished around the British coast other boats always called you up on the radio by using your boat's name, but in the Clyde for some reason it is usual to call you up by your boat's number. In our case the boats number was ignored, and we became known as 007 "i.e. licensed to kill" because of the time in which we completed our port to home and return journeys. I always did all the driving myself and was normally accompanied by soundly sleeping crewmen who obviously had complete confidence in the competence of their driver. One of the most extreme car trips that I ever undertook occurred while we were fishing at Inverness for sprats. We were out in the firth and had just filled our boat with fish and were about to shoot the net again to catch some more for our partner boat. When I engaged the gear and throttle lever to move ahead the engine instantly speeded up but the propeller failed to turn. Obviously we had some type of gearbox problem. I went below into the engine room only to find no obvious fault so that meant that there must be an internal failure within the gear box. Being unable to continue fishing all we could do was get a tow from our partner boat back to the harbour. Once moored up I left the two crews to start unloading while I went off to the fish salesman's office to phone our insurance company and notify them of the problem. I then contacted our local service engineers who normally carried out all of our repair work but they informed me that they did not carry any spare parts for this particular type of gear box and that they thought it would be best if I contacted the main service company in Norwich for their advice. I then telephoned his company and spoke with the chief service engineer. He advised that the best solution would be if I could bring the gear box to their facility in Norwich. He would then guarantee that it would be fully serviced and repaired within one working day. I told them to expect to see me at their door when they arrived for work the next morning. I went back on board the boat and immediately set about removing the gearbox. Once this was accomplished we manoeuvred it up through the hatch onto the deck and lifted it with our derrick on to the quayside where it was loaded into my car.

It was four thirty in the afternoon when I set off on my journey. This meant that I was going to be caught up in the worst of teatime traffic. Nevertheless I hammered down the road to Stonehaven as quickly as possible. After grabbing something to eat I transferred the gearbox into my parents' car which was a Renault Gordini that was faster and more powerful than my own vehicle. The total distance from Inverness to Norwich is approximately 592 miles but I was parked up at the entrance to their workshops well before opening time in the morning. Once they had gone off with the gearbox I parked up in the quietest corner of their car park. There I reclined my seat and slept soundly till just after 4pm when I was wakened by one of their men banging on the car roof and informing me that my gearbox was ready. As soon as the gearbox was loaded in the car I set off on the return journey, first to Stonehaven to change vehicles and then on to Inverness. We transferred the gearbox onto the boat and I had it reinstalled and ready for sea by six o'clock in the morning. Feeling pretty exhausted we set off to sea for a hard day's work. Looking back now I realize I was mad, but at that time my only concern was that the livelihood of a total of 10 families depended on me getting my boat repaired and back to work in the shortest possible time. Quite a few years later while working with my second much bigger Bahati we were involved in pair trawling for mackerel in Cornwall. We regularly used to drive all the way from Aberdeen to Penzance and return once a fortnight. We normally completed this approximately seven hundred mile journey in just under 11 hours including two stops along the way for meals, refreshment and refuelling. I did all the driving, while normally my five crewmen slept soundly between stops.

Inverness and Cambeltown were not the only locations that we fished from with Bahati. On several years once sprat fishing had come to an end at Inverness we sailed south with our pair partner to the waters of the Firth of

Forth. The sprat fishery there normally took place from mid-February until the early spring and we normally landed catches in Granton on the Edinburgh side of the firth or at BurntIsland on the Fife Coast. There were never the same large number of boats involved in this fishery as compared to the Moray Firth but it did afford us the opportunity of working in more sheltered waters until the weather conditions improved in the late spring.

The composition of the annual sprat landings caught in all these coastal waters over the years were relatively constant. 90% of the sprats landed were very immature fish less than one year old. The next 7% of the catch were made up of one and two year old fish. The final 3% of the sprats caught were large mature fish that were capable of spawning and ensuring the future survival of the sprat stock. The vast majority of the mature sprat stock never ventured into coastal waters. They remained far from the shore out in the open North Sea. All those mature sprats gathered to spawn out in the central North Sea in midsummer. Up until the advent of the purse-seine no one had ever been tempted to exploit this mature fish stock. This fish stock over the years had acted like capital in the bank, and the catches we inshore boats made never amounted to more than taking the interest on this capital. These coastal fisheries had been going on for generations without affecting the size of the stock. To be able to catch these immature sprats we had to deploy nets with bags of less than 14 mm mesh size. Suddenly in its wisdom the then labour government decided that we would all have to adopt a minimum mesh size of 16 mm enabling 90% of any potential catch to escape and thus render this traditional fishery completely unviable at the stroke of a pen. There was to be a derogation clause to this new order however. The then new and increasing fleet of large purse seiners were to be allowed to continue using the smaller mesh nets. How fair and justifiable a piece of legislation could this be? All fisheries legislation in Parliament is normally made simply by placing a copy of any proposed order in the library of the house of commons. Unless a sufficient number off MPs lodge a prayer against this order, the order becomes law. On this occasion I managed to persuade my local MP Sir Alex Buchanan Smith to pray against the order and he in turn got enough other fishing constituency MPs to add their names to the list. When this happens the government has to announce a period for consultation, and then a select committee debate is held to confirm or deny the passage of the order. The government always has the right to maintain a proportional majority of the number of members on any committee. I became very involved with other skippers around the coast who were to be affected by this impending legislation. We all tried to stir up as much news coverage as possible in our local areas to gain support for our cause. The two sprat bags that I owned had cost me over a thousand pounds each would become illegal and would have to be destroyed with no possible compensation. My first action was to get the two local fisheries officers to come along and officially measure my nets. I got them to confirm in writing that my nets had both failed to comply with the proposed new minimum size legislation. My local MP Sir Alec Buchanan Smith then took my case to the parliamentary ombudsman seeking for him to review the situation. Some days later I was invited to go to London to meet with the ombudsman to explain the grounds of my complaint. He was very understanding and at first glance thought I had a strong case. I was therefore very surprised when several days later two senior fisheries officers from the department's headquarters in Edinburgh came to see me and to re-examine my nets. These superior officers then informed me that a mistake had been made and that my nets now did indeed comply with the law. They gave me a letter confirming this fact. A week or so later I received a letter from the parliamentary ombudsman advising me that it had been his intention to rule in my favour but now that he had been advised by the department that my nets were now in compliance with the law he would have to drop the action as there was no case to answer. This was to be the first time that I was to discover personally just how devious our government departments and ministers could be when seeking their own way.

A couple of weeks later the date for the parliamentary committee debate was set and my MP suggested that he would set up a meeting with all the interested fisheries MPs on the day before the debate. He requested that I should go along and explain the situation to them preferably in the company of another affected skipper from a different area. I agreed to take part in this meeting and managed to get the sprat committee chairman of the Northumberland fisherman's Association to go along with me and make the case for his area. I had never been to the Houses of Parliament before and was virtually goggle-eyed in these austere surroundings. Sir Alex led us up stairs and along corridors until finally coming to a committee room door which he opened and ushered us in. I was to find myself on the raised platform at the end of the chamber looking down on the faces of some thirty plus members of Parliament. Sir Alex called the meeting to order and introduced me explaining that I was one of his constituents who would be very badly affected if the proposed legislation were to be introduced. It was then my turn to address the assembled MPs. It's amazing how dry one's mouth can become at moments like these. It is not the sort of situation that most fishing skippers expect to find themselves in. As I stood up and started to make my presentation I happened to glance at the wall clock at the other end of the chamber and noted the time. I finally finished speaking some thirty-five minutes later. I could not believe that I had been allowed to speak uninterrupted for so long. I was even more amazed to be given some applause when I sat down. Whether it was merited or was simply relief that I had finished, I was not sure. Many of the members then left, but those who were to be taking part in the debate on the following day stayed on and we had an ongoing discussion for more than an hour. I was invited to come to the debate the following day and sit in the public benches beyond the barrier at the end of the chamber. They explained to me that if they had any questions that they were unsure about during the debate, it would be possible for them to leave the chamber by bowing to the chair and passing out through the barrier and therefore out of the debating chamber. Once out of the chamber they were free to come and sit by me so that I could help them with any technical problems. During these committee debates the government has all their advisers at hand but the opposition members are not allowed to receive any advice from within the chamber. Next morning I met up with Sir Alex in the Westminster lobby and he led me along to the committee room where the debate was to take place, guiding me to a seat on a bench very close to the gap in the barrier that would allow the members to access and exit the chamber. The committee members were finally all in place and the meeting was called to order and the debate began. Hugh Brown the then Scottish Secretary of State was leading the debate for the government and delivered his prepared statement. Sir Alex, Alan Beith and other opposition MPs set about destroying his case. His official government advisers were frantically shuffling and searching files and passing down notes to allow the Minister to continue in the face of this withering assault. In the meantime I had as many as three committee members at any one time leaving the chamber and coming to sit by me in the public benches to get statistical advice as to how they could trump the Minister's aces. When the debate was finally concluded and a vote was taken the government even with its built-in majority was defeated. This was the first time in that parliament that the government had been defeated in a committee debate. The committee members started to leave the chamber and I was more than a little surprised when Alan Beith the Liberal MP came and shook my hand and said "Congratulations I hope you realize that you had a major hand in preparing all of our speeches and arguments in this chamber today". Sir Alex then waved to me to enter the chamber and come and meet the government minister. Through Sir Alex I had been conducting a vitriolic postal debate with the Scottish Secretary of State for many weeks. Now we were about to meet face-to-face. If looks could kill that was the moment I should have died, but instead I shook hands with him and said "Yes I am the bastard who has caused you all this trouble". We then started to conduct a reasonable discussion about the pros and cons of any change in the law and at this point we were joined by the then chief fisheries officer for Scotland, a Mr MacLeod. I had in my briefcase two sample squares of my 14 mm sprat netting. One square was made up of knotted net while the other was constructed of machine woven knotless net. I explained to the minister that these were samples of my nets that had first been failed and then remarkably passed after their re-examination by more senior fisheries department officials. The chief fisheries officer then went to his briefcase and took out his official Northeast Atlantic net measuring gauge. I gave him the knotted sample of net first and by using a really excessive amount of force he was able to force the gauge through the mesh, immediately announcing "There you go, that passes". I then gave him the square of net of knotless construction which he then tried to force the gauge through. Only after he had turned almost red with the effort did anything happen. But he had not passed the gauge through the mesh but on each occasion that he tried he had simply broken a leg of the mesh and therefore the net must be adjudged to fail the test. I then said "Excuse me Mr Chief Fisheries Officer but I think that you will find in your proposed new legislation it clearly states that the official 16mm by 2 mm net gauge must be able to pass freely through any mesh. I do not consider that in any way doing what you have just demonstrated could be interpreted as allowing the official gauge to pass freely through the mesh." There was a deadly silence which brought the conversation to a close with red faces among several of the officials on the government side. That summer I regret to say most of the large new purse seine operating fishing boats descended for the first time ever on the spawning stock of mature sprats in the central North Sea and virtually wiped them out. There were big write-ups in the fishing press regaling just how much fish these boats were capturing. The most tragic part of this story was that all the fish caught were going to make fish meal, because the oil content of these spawning fish at this time of year was too high for it to be of any food manufacturing use. We were never able to return to any major winter sprat fisheries after that wasteful summer slaughter.

Chapter 5

Shortly after experiencing the events in the last chapter I decided that I would have to review my situation and methods of working if I was to remain financially viable. Quite a few new bigger and more powerful boats were now fishing alongside us on our normal fishing grounds. This was exerting a considerable pressure on our ability to make a viable catch in the relatively short time that we could remain at sea, with our ever present constraint of keeping our catch in the best condition. We knew from experience that we had to land our catch every second day to ensure that all of our fish caught were landed in the best possible condition. We were landing our catches into the fish market at Aberdeen. This was a port covered by the dock labour regulations and was unionised to the maximum. To land your catch here you were forced to employ official dock labour in the shape of fish porters. Dependent on your catch size you were allocated a gang of men to unload your catch. As if it was not bad enough being forced to employ high-cost labour to unload you own catch, which you were perfectly capable and prepared to land with your own crew, you had to pay for this affliction whether you chose to use them or not. As if this in itself was not a bad enough unnecessary cost, these gangs of men had traditionally been allowed to take home some fish from your catch, referred to as "fries", supposedly for their own domestic use. This privilege had gone totally out of control and because of the union power nobody seemed to be prepared to challenge what was going on. If you were allocated five fish porters to land your catch, you would invariably find that four men would be unloading your catch while the fifth man would be sitting on an upturned fish box filleting the selected best and most valuable large lemon soles from your catch to bag up and make up into the labourers' "Fries". It was a complete racket. As these men could be employed on as many as five additional boats making landings on any one morning, the amount and value of fish that was walking off the market each day could only be guessed at. Certainly most of the abducted fish seldom found its way home for any so called domestic use. It was sold on to previously contracted third parties in the catering trade, ensuring that a not inconsiderable tax-free bonus was made each day by the fish porters involved.

My worst experience of these activities that I personally endured happened on a day that we were landing what for us was a very big catch of cod. In total we had caught about one hundred and thirty boxes, virtually as much as much as our boat could carry. We found ourselves by chance berthed at the fish market between two large steel trawlers that were landing their catches after being more than 10 days at sea. Because of the size of our catch we had been obliged to employ nine fish porters, as on this occasion we were landing a few boxes more than the demarcation line for requiring only five men. Worse still I discovered that two men were employed on filleting at least two hundred weight of our most valuable sole to make up the "fries" for all the fish porters employed on the two large trawlers along with the men on our boat. These men were very selective in their choice of fish. Their regular buyers for their "fries" just did not want to buy up to ten day old fish off the large trawlers. Two boxes of large soles virtually stolen, even in those days,was worth more than a hundred pounds to us. On this occasion I went directly to the dock labour employers to make an official complaint, but got absolutely no satisfaction. The manager merely gave a shrug of his shoulders and said, "What can we do? If we say anything they'll all be out on strike and bring the entire market to a close". On that particular day if we had taken the official cost of employing the nine fish porters and divided it equally between myself and my two crew men we would have been in receipt of a payment greater than our actual wages were for working two days at sea and making the catch.

In addition to these ridiculous costs on dock labour the unionisation of all the labour force in all other dockside service sectors became just as bad. The oil industry was beginning to come to the fore in Aberdeen and qualified engineers in every sector could find ready work in the oil sector. Employers were frightened to say anything to their workers because they knew that if they upset them they would just walk off and get a job offshore. All the boats normally wanted to get any service jobs attended to at the weekend but in unionised Aberdeen harbour if you wanted a job undertaken on a Saturday or Sunday and you had to pay overtime rates not just for the man that you required but for two further men in addition, because there had to be a team of at least three men before they were allowed to go aboard a boat. Even if the engineer only needed about an hour to complete his work you had to pay the overtime rate of these three men for a full half shift more than a hundred pounds minimum labour charge on any job. Our small enterprise obviously just could not stand this scale of overheads. This simply could not go on, we had to change to a new way of working or we would go burst. After a great deal of thought I decided that I would take the boat up to Burghead on the Moray Firth and change our method of fishing to trawling for prawns.

We purchased the necessary trawl doors and two prawn trawls with their required sweeps etc. and set sail for Burghead thinking that this was to be our last chance of making a success of our small boat. On arrival at Burghead we discovered a fleet of more than 20 boats of own size working out of this small harbour. To us this looked very promising because we reckoned that if they were all making a living here, surely we would be able to do the same. The Misty Isle our earlier partner boat at sprat fishing was still prawn trawling amongst this fleet. Willie Slater the skipper readily agreed to give me copies of all the Decca-navigator positions of known wrecks and hazards in the area. He further suggested that we should tow our first few hauls alongside his boat and in this way we would quickly find if our gear was operating satisfactorily, and was making catches of a comparable quantity to the amount of prawns his boat was catching. We were able to find our feet very quickly in this type of fishing, and were pleasantly surprised to find how much more money we were able to make in our weekly pay packets from so much less physical effort. We were only going to sea for six or seven hours at most on any night during the summer. That for a start meant we were only having to buy a little more than a quarter of the fuel that we required in our old fishery. In addition to this we did not have any of the dreaded dock labour charges to pay. This in itself was a major saving. Perhaps the gross value of our catches had fallen but they were certainly leaving us with much better wages and a good profit margin for

the boat to help meet our repayments and cover the costs of maintenance and improvements. After about the first six months fishing for prawns we had enough money to allow us to convert our winch to a full trawl specification using wire trawl warps instead of the ropes we had been using up until this time. This measure in turn made our operation much more efficient and resulted in a further increase in our fishing ability. Being based at Burghead also made it much easier for us to keep an eye out for any appearance of sprat shoals coming into the area. After mid-November when there was a good possibility of sprats entering the area one or other of the boats in the local fleet would spend a day sailing up into the three firths farther west to check whether there were any sprats present. In early December there was some evidence that some fish had arrived and so we teamed up with a slightly larger boat that was working in Burghead but whose crew came from Arbroath in Angus. On the following Sunday night having loaded our sprat gear we set off towards the inner Moray Firth while searching all the way west with our echo sounder in the hope of finding some sprats. There was not much evidence of fish to be seen
until we entered the Beauly Firth up beyond Inverness where we did encounter some positive signs and were able to shoot our net and catch enough fish to make a landing. Once we had started fishing in the inner firth we were able to continue on fishing there until the beginning of February. Because of the scarcity of sprats in the Inverness Firth on many occasions we had to venture further afield and sail out of the Inverness Firth and on to the Cromarty Firth. On most occasions we found the sprat shoals there to be well up beyond Invergordon,

frequently in the area where the new road bridge now crosses the firth. On one occasion when we ventured into this firth we had not been able to find any fish and darkness was falling, so we decided to spend the night at Invergordon harbour. We were told by the pier master that we should go around to the inshore side of the piled pier because they were expecting a very large fleet auxiliary tanker to enter the port and moor up on the outer side of the pier at high water. We had all gone to our beds and were sound asleep when we were wakened by our boat banging up against the piles of the pier as the giant tanker was nudged into position and moored up only yards from us. We all got up and went on deck to watch the performance as several mooring lines and wire mooring ropes were taken ashore and secured. Finally the operation was completed and the big ship shut down its engines and peace once more descended on the harbour. We went back to bed to get some more shuteye before dawn would bring a start to another day's labour. Several hours later we were wakened by people crossing our deck, and much shouting and conversations in foreign languages. We wondered what the hell was going on so I went up on deck to investigate. I was amazed to discover the underside of the pier and all the pier piles were being swarmed over by a flock of Chinese deckhands off the large tanker. It was nearly low tide by now and so they had plenty of space to clamber around. They were all wearing head torches with bags or baskets on their backs and it turned out that they were catching any living birds that had chosen to roost amongst the pier supports that night. They finished up with three big basketsful of our assorted feathered friends that were quickly hauled aboard the big ship and carried off in the direction of the galley. There was great glee amongst all the spidermen as the eastern crew men returned to their ship obviously thinking of the feast to come. There were never enough sprats to encourage many other boats to come to the area and leave any other type of fishing that they were currently involved with. I think that that year a maximum of only four pairs of boats at any one time were the most that we saw working in the firth. This was considerably less than the number of boats traditionally involved in this area before the purse-seiners had decimated the spawning stock of the mature sprats in the central North Sea a couple of years previous. As the Inverness fishing drew to a close our Arbroath friends told us that there was a growing fishery in the Firth of Forth and so we fuelled up and sailed off down to that firth and managed to remain in that area fishing for sprats until mid April when we returned to Burghead.

One of the best areas for fishing for prawns off Burghead was known locally as The Barrows. This was nothing to do with a road worker's or gardener's barrow but it had become known by this name because of the number of four wheeled naval mine carriages that were found there. They said that it had been a naval minefield during the war, serving to help to protect the major naval anchorage in the deep sheltered waters of the Cromarty Firth and the naval base at Invergordon. Once the war was over, this protective minefield was supposed to have been swept clean of live mines before the area was used as a dump for many surplus mine carriages and also some surplus inactivated and supposedly safe naval mines. In the forties and fifties this area had never been fished because the prawn fishery had not been developed at that time and no viable quantities of whitefish ever frequented this area. As the prawn fishery developed however the local trawlers kept catching the mine carriages and bringing them ashore to Burghead because if your net was badly damaged by this government dumped material you could be entitled to a degree of compensation. Occasionally one of the local boats would catch a mine and they would then tow it into shallow water in Burghead bay and alert the coast guard and then a bomb and mine disposal team would be sent up from the navy depot at Rosyth to identify the type of mine that had been caught. They then normally exploded the device with fragmentation charges so that it would be of no further danger. In our time at Burghead we caught more than our fair share of mines and we became fairly blasé about them until one day when we caught a mark seventeen mine complete with its laying carriage. This type of mine looked for all the world like a torpedo that was resting on its carriage at an angle of forty five degrees. This mine looked to be in a very corroded state but it was far too heavy for us to take on board. I thought if I tried to tow it into shallow water that there would be a very good chance that it could completely destroy my net. I therefore decided to lower it to the seabed still inside my net but on the end of a heavy rope so that we could haul it up to the surface once the bomb and mine disposal people arrived at the harbour. Having detached our net and lowered it complete with mine to the seabed, we secured a large float to the end of the rope keeping it visible on the surface. We then headed to the harbour and landed our prawns having already contacted the coastguard by radio and advised them about what we had caught and where we had left it. We then had our breakfast and went to bed to have a few hours sleep before the bomb and mine disposal people would arrive. After lunchtime we were wakened by the sound of the loud siren of the approaching emergency vehicle. The naval officer and his team came onboard and we gave him a detailed description of what we had caught. He was very nonchalant about the situation and said that quite a few of that type of mine had been inactivated and dumped near the area we had been working. His crew in the meantime had launched their inflatable boat and loaded all their diving gear and boxes of explosives and detonators onto our boat. Meanwhile a large crowd had gathered on the quayside to watch what was going on. We cast off and left the harbour towing his rubber boat and made for the position where we had left our net with its contents lying on the seabed. We quickly spotted our float and picked it up and started to heave up on the rope with the heavy weight of the mine causing our relatively small boat to list quite markedly. Once the end of the mine reached the surface the officer gave it a quick inspection and declare that it was totally safe and had been one of the dumped ordinance. He suggested that if we put a lifting sling around the mine and lifted it with our derrick as far out of the water as we could it would enable his men to enter the water and try to untangle out nets from the mine with the least possible damage. We agreed to his suggestion and started heaving up on our fish derrick raising the mine slowly out of the water until only about the last 3 feet of its length was left under the surface. His divers then managed to free our net and we succeeded in hauling it aboard. The officer then said that they would attach the demolition charges to the mine along with the detonators before we lowered the mine back to the seabed. His men quickly completed their task of attaching explosives and detonators while a reel of detonation wire was attached to the explosives. We slowly began to lower the mine back down to the seabed while the sailors simultaneously paid out the detonation wire. Three of his men went aboard their inflatable boat along with the necessary equipment for detonating the explosives. The officer told us to retreat away from this position for at least a mile. The officer in the meantime contacted the coastguard and air traffic control at the nearby RAF Kinloss airbase by radio and advised them that an explosion was about to take place. Once he had clearance that all was in order from the onshore people involved, he radioed to his men that they could detonate the mine. We saw the inflatable boat suddenly take off and speed quickly away from the site. Moments later we heard the loud clump of the underwater explosion with the surface over the explosion site rising up like a small hill while the central waterspout continued going up to over 100 feet in the air. This was spectacular enough but then suddenly the whole surface of the sea over the explosion to an area of about the size of a football field erupted into a mass of white hot flame and continued to burn for several minutes. The naval officer in charge of the disposal turned very pale. With many profanities he announced that that F****ing thing must have been live and had in fact been full of phosphorus to set fire to any detonating ship. It began to dawn us just how precarious a situation we had been in while we were holding the mine suspended from our derrick and it was gently rolling backwards and forwards on the edge of our boat's rail. If the old and corroded mine casing had happened to rupture and allowed access to the air the phosphorus would have ignited and without doubt we could all have fried. Over the next several years we caught quite a few more mines but I was always very wary particularly of any mark 17 that we captured just in case it was another live one. On another occasion while fishing about 5 miles west of Burghead we slowed down very abruptly indicating that we had picked up a heavy weight in our net. We heaved ourselves back on our winch and just managed to retrieve the trawl doors and secure them to the rails. We then started hauling in on the sweeps. These are the combination wire and poly fibre ropes that are attached between the trawl doors and the net. We managed to get the end of the net up to the boat's rail, but the object in the net was too heavy for us to be able to haul it any further . We had a rope running from the toe of the net to the centre of the footrope to assist us in hauling the net on board. I decided to heave up on this rope to see if I could find out what the heavy object in our net was. You have to remember that we were working at night in the dark and so the underwater vision was very poor. Suddenly out of the murk we saw the unmistakable shape of a spherical mine complete with its detonation horns which where protruding ominously through the meshes of our net. I immediately started lowering the net and the mine back down into the water so that it couldn't accidentally bump into our boat hull and get detonated if it was a live mine. I thought as the ends of the net were secured to the rails of our boat that I would be safe to engage forward gear and gently tow the object in mid-water in the direction of Burghead harbour to be closer to port when the bomb and mine disposal squad arrived. However whenever I engaged the gear the engine stopped indicating that we had caught up either the footrope or net in our propeller. We were now unable to move under our own power, so there was nothing for it but to lay our anchor so that we didn't get carried off by the tide or wind and find ourselves in any further difficulties. When we were securely anchored I called up the coastguard and informed them of our position and situation. They seemed to get singularly alarmed and immediately all flying was stopped from the nearby airbase and then they inquired if we wanted to be a lifted off by helicopter. I graciously declined the offer and told him that we would go to bed and have a good sleep until such time as the navy bomb disposal team appeared. They appeared to be rather taken aback by this casual attitude but then they had not been fishing from Burghead and developing the track record for catching mines that we now enjoyed. Just after lunchtime the bomb and mine disposal team along with their equipment were delivered on board by helicopter. The helicopter then disappeared off into the distance with a puff of smoke, as if by magic. The officer then requested that we haul up the mine close to the surface so that his divers could see it without the danger of getting entangled in the net. This we accomplished and the divers were able to tell him that it was a brand-new practice mine that had been laid only a couple of weeks earlier during a naval exercise. He then told us it was perfectly safe to bring it up alongside the boat and eventually with their assistance we managed to get it on board by using both our fore and aft lifting derricks in unison. His divers then went down and cleared the obstruction from our propeller allowing us to get the net hauled aboard and set off for Burghead. The mine appeared to us to be huge and when on deck the top of the mine casing was well over the roof of our wheelhouse. The weight was such that the deck on the side of the boat that the mine was on was level with the water while we had to use our hands to assist us climbing up the sloping deck to the other side of the boat. The officer had radioed ashore to the airbase when we got underway to arrange for them to send down a crane to lift the monster ashore and arrange for a lorry to transport it away. When we reached the harbour we found that the police had the whole area cordoned off because it seems that nobody had bothered to inform them that it was a practice rather than a live mine we were bringing ashore. The local north east newspapers had the photograph of our boat with the mine on deck on the front page the following day with the headline "Stonehaven mine sweeping skipper does it again."

During our time at Burghead we had continued to have periodic disasters with our British manufactured boat engine. These all meant lost sea time and expensive repair bills. Despite this we had managed to gather some funds together and we made an application to the White Fish Authority for financial assistance to replace our engine with a much more reliable unit. After waiting for some time approval came through and we sailed our boat down the coast to the harbour at Fraserburgh to allow a marine engineering firm based there to carry out the replacement contract. This contract included fitting a larger propeller shaft and a bigger propeller. In addition hydraulic steering was fitted along with changes in the driving mechanism of our winch. In all the work took a total of three months but cost more than two and a half times what the boat had cost to build originally. Once we got the boat back and restarted fishing we never lost another day's fishing time due to mechanical failure. The

Swedish 120 hp Volvo engine that we fitted ran faultlessly for the four year period up until the launch of my new bigger boat, and to the best of my knowledge continued to operate faultlessly for more than 4 years in the hands of the new owners who had purchased my small Bahati from me. I lost track of where the old boat went after that time.

Our Chapter 6.

In this same year I happened to see an advertisement in the fishing news offering for let by the crown commissioners the small salmon fishing station at Hopeman, a small village only about 2 miles away on the east side of Burghead. The local ship chandler that we purchased all of our gas and gear from had his shop and stores situated on the quayside there. Over the previous couple of years I had become very friendly with the owner of the business and so I went across to see him with the suggestion that it might be worthwhile putting in an offer for the salmon fishing. I learned that the fishery there had not been operated for many years and had never historically been a particularly good fishery. I suggested to my friend that in the circumstances it might be worth putting in a ridiculously low offer just in case no serious offers were made. Unbelievably about a fortnight after the closing date for offers we received confirmation from the crown estates that our offer had been accepted and we could now fish for salmon on this strip of coast using any or all of the legal methods. We found it amazing that our token offer should have been accepted, but we would now be able to fish here legally for the next ten years. We at once set about obtaining the gear that we would require to start fishing for salmon when the legal netting season opened. We had no intention in operating a fully commercial operation but we saw it simply as a way of earning some extra cash in the summer time and it would also mean that if they wanted to assist, my boat crew could make some extra cash as well. The salmon fishing fitted in very well with our summertime working pattern. We normally would be at sea fishing for prawns all night but were well able to do a few hours work on the salmon fishing during the day. We were surprised to find that very soon the salmon fishing far from being just a hobby began to be a serious commercial enterprise. I personally was spending so much time on this enterprise that some of the local skippers started to suggest that I worked all night at the prawns, and all day at the salmon and only went home at the weekend to sleep.

A major problem very soon became obvious with the salmon fishery. Our catches were being virtually decimated by the ravages of the local grey seal population. Our legal and widely used traditional Scottish salmon bag nets were constantly under attack by the seals and we were losing a high percentage of our catch. To try to combat these attacks I applied for a firearms certificate so that I could try to shoot some of the marauding animals and possibly frighten away others. Despite having a track record of having a wide experience of firearms and their safe use during my years in Africa, and in addition having absolutely no convictions even for a motoring offence in the UK. It still took several months before my firearms certificate was finally granted. I could not understand why it was taking so long but then the penny finally dropped. Gordonston School had their boathouse at Hopeman harbour and had sailing cutters on the sea almost every day, whilst conducting other exercises on the beaches and cliffs. The royal princes, Andrew and Edward, were pupils at Gordonston in those years and I suppose somebody patrolling the beach with a very high power rifle complete with telescopic sight was going to be a bit of an issue. When I finally got my rifle the first thing I did at the start of any fishing season was to make myself known to the royal protection squad officer who happened to be in attendance at that particular time. I spent many hours on the shore in the company of some of these men while their charges the princes were out at sea and I would be sitting waiting for a seal's head to pop up at our nets to allow me a shot at it.

While I was experiencing the problem with grey seals at a personal level. I was shortly to learn about the concerns that the marine scientists were expressing about the exploding seal population. For some time I had occasionally been asked to take some of the marine scientists from the fisheries research laboratory in Aberdeen out to sea with us so that they could monitor the ongoing situation as regards the catches of prawns and discard rates from the catches of any other species. It was from one of these marine scientists that I first heard about a high-powered committee of ecologists and prominent scientists who had been studying the effects of the grey seals on the marine fisheries for nearly 20 years. He told me that a report was shortly to be published recommending that over a period of time the grey seal population had to be reduced in number annually until the safe sustainable population of grey seals recommended by this scientific committee was reached. He told me that the scientists had found that the British grey seal population was already consuming more fish annually to keep themselves alive than the British fishing fleet was allowed to catch. I was already experiencing personally their direct effect on our coastal salmon fishing but I had no idea about the wider implication of the scourge of the steadily increasing seal population. Once I was alerted to this fact I started to do some serious research into this situation because this was not only going to affect me but could and would have long-term effects on the British fishing industry.

The grey seals historically had only two predators, killer whales and man. Man had historically always been the principal predator. The grey seals were the only animal to give birth to their pups in late autumn or early winter. The young white-coated pups then had to remain ashore on the exposed breeding beaches for about six weeks, while totally dependent on their mothers rich milk for support until they could go to sea. The vulnerability of the seal pups in this condition had been looked upon as a gift from god from the early days of man. They simply had to go down to the beaches and kill and skin enough seals to clothe and feed their dependents through the coming winter. Excavations from the ancient middens at historically inhabited coastal sites all around the coasts have revealed much evidence of this fact. While early written history also tells us of how beneficial this annual harvest was, it also explains how the range of the grey seals had been reduced until the only successful breeding colonies were to be found in the more exposed and inaccessible areas around the British coast. There was never any suggestion of any over exploitation of this natural resource until the late 1800s when with the advent of superior firearms and the explosion in the international fur trade brought about a dramatic decline in a seal numbers. The British grey seals became the first mammal in history to be offered legal protection status by the British government in 1912. It was stated in Westminster that it was believed that there were only some 500 grey seals remaining on the British coast. These were to be found principally on the island of Rona out in the North Atlantic northwest of Cape Wrath. With this total protection the seal numbers rapidly increased and by 1932 the very eminent Scottish and internationally recognised ecologist, Frank Fraser Darling, was advising the Scottish nature conservancy that grey seal numbers had increased to such an extent that the introduction of licensed hunting to control their numbers should be considered. Although this recommendation was noted no action was taken at that time and then along came the war years and the years up until the early 1950s. The Government Marine scientists finally became so concerned about this ticking time bomb that they persuaded the government into setting up a seal research program to calculate once and for all just how many seals our British coastal waters could support without adversely affecting our fish stocks. This eminent group of scientists and ecologists having studied the program for twenty years finally made their report to the government. The report basically stated that the seal population had reached an unacceptably high level and was adversely affecting our stocks of both whitefish and salmon. They made a recommendation that a target number of mature female seals with their pups should be culled annually over a period of years until the seal population had been gradually reduced to the proposed optimum sustainable level. The government were well aware of the sentimental backlash that would come from the "bunny hugging city dwellers" and nature lovers who had no knowledge of the scientific reasoning for this cull. Seals to them were tiny white cuddly things that could do no wrong. All sections of the media immediately jumped on the bandwagon of protest, not bothering to look into the scientific facts that justified the proposed cull. To the so-called nature conservation organizations this was like manna from heaven and with plenty of television coverage constantly showing films of the Canadian seal hunt with baby seals and plenty of blood on the white snow and ice, cash flowed in to support these organizations like never before. Harold Wilson was the Prime Minister and his government instructed the fish dependent organizations not to enter the fray or take part in any debate. He stated that the need for the seal cull had been scientifically proven and it was definitely going to go ahead. Unfortunately there was a by-election pending in a Greater London constituency and the labour government only had a wafer thin majority. They became very concerned that the seal issue might be enough to lose them the seat in this urban constituency. At lunchtime on the day that the cull was called off Harold Wilson reassured representatives of all the fish dependent organizations that the cull would be starting the following day. Then, on the six o'clock news that evening the cull was called off. The reason given was that there was insufficient evidence to justify the cull. After a 20 year intensive research program by his high powered seals committee just how pathetic an excuse could that be. During the twenty years of the seals research program 813 dead seals had been subject to autopsy examination and it was recorded that 90% of the stomach contents from these seals was made up of pieces of flesh from large commercial species of fish. The scientists conducting these autopsies also recorded that no Otolith bones of these classes of fish were ever found. Otolith bones are a species identifying small bone from the ear of the fish. It was not expected by anybody in the fishing industry that Otolith bones from these large fish species would ever be found in the seals guts because from all the evidence gathered seals did not eat the heads of their large prey species of fish.

After this blatant deception by the government the fishing industry started to fight back but it was now too late to be able to force any political U-turn. A couple of weeks later I found myself being invited down to Birmingham to appear on live television on the popular midday program Pebble Mill at One. It was trailed that I was to be a spokesman advocating the seal slaughter, a subject guaranteed to get good viewing figures. It was first arranged that I should take part in the Wednesday program. But then I got a phone call asking me if I could come on the following Monday instead which I confirmed I was happy to agree to. After doing all the sound tests and dragging me into make up, the producer led me down the stairs into the foyer of the television building from where the program was broadcast. As we descended the stairs she said to me "You do you realize why we kept you back for the Monday program, don't you?" I said I just thought it was something to do with the program schedules. "Oh no," she replied, "This is the English schools midterm break and so we will be assured of at least 5 million viewers today." Rather a disturbing thought just before you are about to broadcast live on your very first television appearance. The program producers had been so sure that the telephone switchboard would be swamped by protesting phone calls after my contribution, that they had arranged for the switchboard staff to take their lunch break early so that they could all be back on duty before the program started. After my introduction I explained about the 20 years scientific research program that had been undertaken before the cull decision was made. I had also taken two mature cod along to the studio that represented the weight of the minimum amount of fish that an adult seal had to eat every day simply to stay alive. In addition I had with me a photograph that they transmitted of a large nine foot long, forty seven stone, dead, bull grey seal, which was suspended vertically by its tail flippers with a man standing alongside it to give the idea of scale. I was able to tell the viewers that this one animal had been found to have 42 pounds of salmon in its stomach when it was examined. I went on to explain that the seal population around Britain already had an annual dietary requirement of fish to keep them alive that was greater than the total amount of fish that the British fishing fleet was allowed to catch annually. I was originally supposed to be on screen for some five minutes but I was informed later that I had actually done 8 1/2 minutes. This does not seem very long but I was told that it was practically unheard of to allow someone to overrun for this length of time. As a result of my broadcast, far from the switchboard being inundated with protest calls, up until five o'clock that evening it had only received some calls in support of the seal cull but they had not received a single phone call of complaint.

If the government had only had the guts to allow the industry to make their presentations and explanations when the scientists first produced their report I personally believe that the great British public would have come to a more balanced view of the real situation as it affected our fish stocks. However left to feed on the diet of sentimental crap that was being served up by all our media at the behest of the so-called environmental lobby, the public were led by the nose sobbing as they went to pay good money to save our seals.

To this day the seal population is still increasing. They are still the major consumer of fish from the sea and nothing has been done about them. In the meantime what the scientists were originally concerned about has come to pass. Fishermen all around Britain have been subject to culling and our fishing fleet has been drastically reduced in size under the pretext of helping in the recovery of our fish stocks. This recovery is never going to happen until something is done about seal predation, because with their constantly increasing population the grey seals can consume any potential increase of our fish stocks. Every grey seal consumes about two and a half tons of fish a year. They only eat fish. They can't live on grass or fresh air.

It was after this initial television appearance that I seemed to be the person who the media called on whenever the subject of grey seal appeared. I found myself frequently on radio and television putting forward the fishermen's case. This was all right up to a point, but I soon found out that the producers and managers of programs in both radio and television like to made their production fit their desired views. You could find yourself being interviewed and recorded explaining the facts of the case rationally and comprehensively only to find that when broadcast only selected bits would be used completely destroying the value of the interview. I simply said, "Enough is enough. If you want me in the future to be part of any program it has got to be live. I will willingly make myself available for a television or radio debate with anybody that you can find who is prepared to confront me on the issue of grey seals and fisheries." They did not like my attitude and tried several times to get me to change my mind. Finally they admitted that they simply could not get any of the overly vocal bunny hugging conservationists to agree to a debate. These people crawl out from under their stones in southern cities occasionally and go out into the wilds for a week so that they can publicise their opinions on nature. I held my ground however determined that I would only debate live. Several months later I was contacted by a major commercial morning television company saying that they had got Mr Brian Davies, the boss of the International Fund for Animal Welfare from Canada, to agree to come to UK to face me in live debate. Would I be prepared to come to the studios in London so that a debate could take place ? "Bring him on" was my response. I had for several years been in regular contact with the Canadian Government through Bob Merner in the Canadian High Commission in London. I was therefore well briefed on who and what Mr Davies was and what the likely extent of his knowledge on grey seals would be.

I had flown down to London the night before the debate because the taxi was to pick me up at my hotel at 5am to take me to the television studios. I think the debate started at about 6.30 but in my opinion it was a none event. Mr Davis is a glorified publicist and was immediately trying to get the debate moved to the blood on the ice Canadian seal hunts as this is where his organisation gets most of their income from. Their money is mainly raised from sobbing housewives conned by his publicity staff after they have fed the media with contrived footage of supposed seal killing. When I pointed out that he was speaking about a different breed of seals on a different continent and that nothing that had ever been considered in this country had any similarity to what he was trying to publicise he was virtually stumped. I then took the chance of explaining the true situation in this country. In 1912 grey seals were the first species of mammals in the world afforded protection by act of parliament when it was recorded that only an estimated 500 grey seals were left in the wild. This original population with protection had now exploded in numbers to the point that they had a food requirement, simply to keep them alive, of more than the British fishing fleet was allowed to catch annually. The British Government were already culling British fishermen with forced decommissioning and restrictive fishing quotas. I stressed that in my opinion it was now about time to introduce the gradual reduction of seal numbers as recommended by the twenty year government research program. He tried to bluster on with some comments but they were easily dealt with as irrelevant. The debate then ended but was repeated twice on that morning's broadcasts before 10am. I received a lot of positive responses supporting my case and the TV company said that they had received a good positive response with no complaints.

That is the only time in my life that I have experienced being stared at by members of the general public as I walked round London looking at the sights to pass the time until I had to go to Heathrow to catch my return flight to Scotland. It was obvious that a high percentage of the people on the streets had seen the morning program and recognised me.

My final confrontation on the grey seals issue came about when I had to go to the EEC parliament in Strasburg and address an important committee there on the effects that grey seals were having on our fish stocks and the viability of our inshore fisheries combined with the proven damage being ravaged on the north Atlantic salmon stocks. To say that it is intimidating to find yourself about to address a large and important major committee in a huge horse-shoe shaped chamber in the parliament is an understatement. A very large Swedish MEP was to chair this meeting and a Norwegian fisheries professor was to be the other speaker. The Swedish chairman led us into the chamber and onto the platform. He placed me at his right hand with the Norwegian professor on his left. Looking out across the chamber I could see all the little glass boxes in the back wall housing the translators to the many languages of the EEC. The chairman showed me how to switch on my microphone when I started speaking and told me to turn it off when I was finished. This would allow other people to ask questions etc. The chairman then called the meeting to order and introduced me as Mr McDonald a fishing skipper from Scotland that was to address them on the issue of the interaction of grey seals and fisheries. I was very well prepared and had much practise in speaking on this issue over the previous years and once the initial nerves were over I found it relatively easy to put across our case. Once I was finished the Norwegian professor took over and went into great detail on the scientific findings on the grey seal issue that confirmed all I had said and told the members present that Norway was very worried about the increasing numbers of grey seals in EEC waters. He explained that Norway and Iceland had for many years conducted an annual seal harvest to ensure that numbers of seals in their waters did not get completely out of control. He was recommending that similar action was required in the EEC. After a lengthy question and answer session the chairman brought the meeting to a close. His final statement will always stay in my mind. He said " I know little about seals but in Sweden we have to kill thousands of elk every year to control their numbers or very quickly there would be no forests or farms as we know them. In nature every animal has a time to die even you ladies and gentle men have a time to die. Thank you".

Chapter 7.

Having got that political tirade off my chest I had better get back to my original story about the fishing. We continued working at the prawns out of Burghead for that summer, very pleased with the fact that we were not constantly having to worry about mechanical breakdowns. Sprat fishing that year was very poor so we had no option but to soldier on catching prawns and whitefish all through the winter. It didn't prove to be very rewarding mainly because of lost sea time due to prolonged spells of bad stormy weather. At least fishing out of Burghead, if there were two or three days of storms forecast, we could get in the car and drive the 90 miles home to enjoy a little comfort until the weather relented and we could go back to sea.

My younger brother Hamish had been employed in the government fisheries department in Aberdeen ever since he left school. He was a fanatical sports enthusiast and a Scottish international badminton player. He had always wanted however to go to sea in his own fishing boat and finally the opportunity occurred and he was able buy a second-hand fishing boat from the Shetland Islands. It was about 55 feet long with a Caterpillar engine and had originally been built in Norway. When he sailed the boat south he took it to Burghead so that he could get used to the vessel and iron out any problems before sailing off to the west coast where he intended to work. There must be a strange hereditary failing in our family because on his very first night at sea fishing with his boat he managed to catch a mine in an area that had never yielded a mine before. Once assured that everything was working properly he set off to the west coast and fished there until early the following summer, then he came back to the east coast to put his boat on the slipway for its annual paint and engine service. When sailing back up to Burghead he happened to come across two pairs of boats fishing about five or six miles off Buckie. There were apparently some shoals of summer herring about over the shallow banks. When he arrived in Burghead he told us about what he had seen and asked if we wanted to take our herring trawl aboard and see if we could catch some of these herring. We quickly put our trawl doors and prawn nets ashore and hauled the herring pair trawl out of our quayside store and aboard the boat before setting off for the shallow water off Buckie as soon as we were ready. Once we got to the area we searched about looking for signs of the herring with our echo sounders. We finally found some traces and shot away our gear and were able to catch some herring. It took about four or five relatively short hauls to catch enough fish to merit going ashore and landing. As this was the height of summer any catch made had to be landed very fresh. This was the first time that I had ever been able to pair trawl for pelagic species of fish at this time of year. Our fishing was short-lived however as after only three landings some teams of big herring pair trawlers arrived from Fraserburgh and they required only one night's work to clean up the entire area of all herring.

We returned to Burghead to revert to our prawn fishing. I continued to work out of Burghead while my brother went east to Buckie and worked with the prawn fleet there until the autumn. By mid-November we had teamed up as a pair again and set about searching for sprats all over the three western firths. There were not a lot of sprats about yet but we were able to make a living. With his boat being so much bigger than ours we generally loaded all the fish into his boat. Only on occasions when we had a really good day's fishing did we need to load any fish into my boat. My brother had managed to arrange for us a fish-buying contract with a Norwegian fish merchant who had his processing premises on the quayside at Inverness. Providing the fish were of suitable quality everything we caught was going for human consumption and that made a big difference to the value of catches. All was going well until 13th November. We had just made a haul down by Munlochie and had caught a good bag full of fish and were lying with the boats lashed together brailing the fish aboard his boat. Each lift of fish that we lifted on board weighed about a ton and a half. A lift of this weight was up in the air swinging over his hatchway about to be released into the hold when there was a sudden crack. The bag of fish fell into the hold and my brother collapsed on the deck. A shackle pin securing one of the 8 inch steel guiding blocks that was supporting the weight of the fish had sheared and the heavy 8 inch block had flown across the deck like a cannonball smashing my brother's leg up against the steel hatch, obviously to his very severe injury. There was a lot of blood and his leg was obviously severely smash just below the knee. I got a tourniquet on his leg as soon as possible to stop or reduce the blood loss. I shouted to a crewman to break up a fish box so that I could use the corner section between the side and bottom boards to form a triangular shaped long splint to secure his leg to try to prevent any movement. I then told the men to get the net hauled over onto my boat while I contacted Wick radio with a PAN message to inform them that I had a very seriously injured man aboard. I informed them that we would be in Inverness Harbour in about forty minutes time. I further advised them that due to the blood loss we would require a doctor and a medical team to be there to give emergency treatment and get the injured man lifted ashore and off to hospital. I left most of the crews on my boat and taking only two crew men with me set off in my brother's boat at full speed for Inverness harbour. The Norwegian fish processor had been listening to our radio conversation in his office and watched us approach the harbour. As there were still no signs of any emergency services arriving, he took it upon himself to call the police to find out what was happening. The person who answered said that they knew nothing about it but would find out. We were moored up at the quayside before any emergency services arrived. The first and only emergency vehicle to arrive was an ambulance with a driver but no medical team and the ambulance wasn't even fitted with the type of stretcher that is require to secure an injured man on to lift him ashore. We simply couldn't hang about with my injured brother in the state he was in. We got the stretcher out of the ambulance and down onto the boat. When my brother was securely tied on to the stretcher we used some lifting slings for our boat's derrick and lifted him ashore like a box of fish and got him into the ambulance and off on his way to hospital. I was in a totally incandescent rage about this complete failure of the local emergency services. Being the bloody-minded person that I am, I was determined to have somebody's guts for garters. I immediately contacted Wick Radio Station and got copies of the timing of my calls to them and their onward calls to the emergency services in Inverness. This was to be my starting point. Before doing anything further I had to go and find my sister-in-law who was teaching in one of the country schools about 8 miles outside Inverness. With some difficulty I found the school and told her as much as I could about the accident and then I went with her to Raigmore Hospital in Inverness. We were unable to find out much about the situation because Hamish was still in the operating theatre. I left my sister-in-law at the hospital and then set off to find the regional medical officer of health to begin my trail of explosions.

When I got to his office I was told that he couldn't meet anyone without an appointment. I told his secretary that he bloody well could and he bloody well would, and if he wasn't prepared to see me immediately I would be going in to see him. Needless to say he appeared threatening to have me removed from the building. In my highly stressed state I think I did very well not to do more than tell him he had better shut up and listen up. I then told him of what had happened and that I knew the messages had been passed to the medical and emergency services by Wick radio but that nothing appeared to have been done. Now several hours later my brother is still in the operating theatre at Raigmore hospital and is hopefully still alive, but with no thanks due to his emergency services. His attitude had changed somewhat by this time and he apologized profusely and said that the matter would be fully investigated.

The following day I went to see the head of the department of marine health and safety in Aberdeen and repeated the full sorry story to him. I explained to him that if I as a skipper of a fishing boat and responsible for the lives for my crew make an emergency call ashore explaining the seriousness of the injuries to a crewman and reporting of major blood loss, I expected that the medical services that I deemed necessary would be in place at the quayside when I got my casualty to the shore. They were horrified with my story and they assured me that they would immediately begin a full investigation. When the investigation was concluded some months later it revealed a sorry tale of incompetence and irregularities. The message was sent from Wick Radio to Inverness all right, but from that point on the supposedly recorded timing and content of the messages were a complete shambles. They promised a better service in future but that was not going to alter our situation. When I went to visit my brother in the hospital the next day I was told by the ward doctor that we had been very lucky, and if we had been delayed much longer in getting my brother to hospital he wouldn't have made it. The A&E team had to start giving him major blood transfusions as soon as they had him in their care. He had already undergone major surgery and would require further surgery in the coming months to try to save his leg. He had his leg in plasterer over 13 months before it really started to heal. They said that he was very lucky to have his leg even if it was now a bit shorter than the other. The doctors cautioned him that he should be able to walk once he was fully recovered but that he must not expect ever to regain anything like full strength and fitness in his injured limb. Hamish however is another bloody-minded McDonald, and when they told him that he could start on a program of physiotherapy and gentle exercise to build up his leg, they didn't realize what they had unleashed. After the first few weeks of the physiotherapy and gentle exercises to start to rebuild his leg he developed into a psychopath and instead of doing the exercises two of three times a day he did the exercises continuously until he neared collapse. At this point he would rest a while and then repeat the exercises again, time after time, repeatedly, all day until reaching the point of almost total exhaustion by the time evening came round. The doctors were amazed by his progress but it was entirely due to his own determination that his recovery was as good as it was. He was not able to continue fishing but became involved in the development of offshore survival training and the building and operation of fast rescue craft. He has now become an acknowledged leading world expert in these fields, having recently been honoured with the awarding of an OBE for services to his country in this field.

Chapter 8.

With Hamish lying in hospital I had to set about finding a skipper to take his boat for a time if we were to be able to keep fishing as a pair. We managed to get the former owner of Hamish's boat to come down from Shetland and take over for a time. The sprat fishing did not prove to be very good but we managed to keep the pair working until the start of the Christmas break. In the meantime Hamish had made the decision to sell his boat because the prognosis for his recovery was not very bright. We therefore sailed Bahati back to Burghead and resumed prawn trawling to see out the rest of the winter. At this time a new small trawler arrived to work out of Burghead. It was called Kadana and belonged to a skipper from Buckie by the name of Joe Aitken. The boat had the same Volvo engine as Bahati and frequently we found ourselves fishing alongside each other and were therefore able to compare catches and satisfy ourselves that our fishing gear was working satisfactorily. Joe and I became quite close friends and so by the time the next sprat season came round we had decided that we would fish as a pair team. We found that we worked very well together and although it wasn't a particularly good sprat season we managed to catch enough to keep us working in the sheltered waters for a good part of the winter. It was at this time that we first began to hear about an English pair of trawlers that were making a great success of pair trawling for whitefish particularly cod. Joe and I started to discuss this subject quite a bit and then we came upon the idea that he might try to get financial backing to allow us to build two nearly identical boats specifically designed for pair trawling either for a pelagic species or whitefish. We both approached the fish selling companies that we dealt with to see whether they would be interested in taking a share interest in the proposed new boats. Both companies were prepared to give us financial backing, and so the next action was to see whether the White Fish Authority would be likely to give us grant and loan assistance for the building of the boats. I don't know whether it was the fact that this was the first time that there had been a proposal to build two almost similar boats specifically designed for pair fishing, but we got our provisional approval granted in a very short time. This allowed us to contact a naval architect and get the boats plans and specifications drawn up. This in turn enabled us to get competitive tenders for the construction of the boats from three boat building companies. In the end it was agreed upon with the approval of the White Fish Authority that Thompson's boatyard at Buckie would build the boats. Mr. Thompson who owned and operated the boatyard said that he would build the two boats in quick succession with the second boat being ready for delivery not more than six months after the first. A coin was tossed to see who would have the first boat and Joe Aitken won. I was not too disappointed about this because being second would allow me the chance of having any minor alterations that I thought beneficial incorporated into my vessel.

While shopping one day in Stonehaven I happened to bump into Bill Dixon, the internationally renowned fishing gear technologist, who had offered me the job as his assistant in FAO that I mentioned earlier in the book. He was now retired from FAO but had been engaged by the Norwegian government fisheries department as an independent fisheries consultant. He was now spending six months each year based in Bergen in Norway. I told him about our plans to build the new boats and immediately he suggested that if my fish selling company and I were in agreement he would happily invest with us in a third share of our partnership. I was more than delighted to think we would have somebody of his calibre and expertise in the team, and the fish selling company were equally pleased to have him join us. So we became a team of three equal partners.

Joe and I had decided that we would have Volvo engines installed in both new boats because we had experienced excellent service from them in our small boats and they were enjoying a high reputation amongst the bigger boats in the fleet that were equipped with them. I had taken the decision to sell the small Bahati as soon as possible to raise funds for the payment of my share of the deposit on a new boat. It was my intention that the salmon fishing could keep me employed through the summer, and if I needed to I could find another job for the winter. The boat was quickly put up for sale but it was to take about 2 1/2 months before the sale was finally completed and I just kept operating the boat until the new owners had finalised the purchase.

It was at this point that Joe and I were told that a representative of the Volvo Swedish engine makers wanted to meet with us at Thompson's boatyard in a couple of days time. When Joe and I arrived at the boatyard at the appointed hour, we found not only the Swedish engine manufacturers' representative but also our naval architect was there to meet with us. The Swedish gentleman opened the meeting by saying how pleased the Volvo company were that we had decided to have our new bigger boats fitted with Volvo engines after having had years of previous experience of Volvo engines in our old boats. He went on to say that the Swedish company engineers thought our boat design and the fact that we were building a pair of almost identical boats with the intention of pair trawling was at that time a unique idea. Their company engineers however thought that our boats were slightly underpowered and that they would be much more efficient boats if we fitted more horsepower. He then went on to make us the offer that Volvo would give us the bigger engines that their engineers recommended at no extra cost to us if we would agree to have them installed in our boats. He went on to say that they thought that this would make our boats much more efficient and as such Volvo would be able to make good use of our boats and their future operating efficiency when advertising engine sales. I immediately thanked him very much for their generous offer but went on to explain that Joe and I have had to invest everything we possessed to be able to get the boats built. The offer of the larger engines was undoubtedly very generous but would result in Joe and I having to find a lot more money that we simply didn't have, to cover the additional charges. I went on to explain to him that bigger horse power meant a heavier propeller shaft and a larger stern tube bearing. As well as the bigger propeller required, this in turn would need a larger Kort nozzle propeller housing along with bigger fuel tanks. All of these additions would have to be costed out, but I was not overly hopeful that Joe and I would be able to raise the finance required however generous to us their offer undoubtedly was. The Swedish gentleman sat quietly for a moment or two and looked towards our boat builder and naval architect. He then stood up and asked Mr. Thompson if he could use a telephone and he was shown through into another office so that he could make his phone call in private. He was on the phone for quite some time but when he reappeared he had a wide smile on his face and told us that he had just been authorized by his company to make his offer inclusive of all these additional charges. Needless to say he was almost knocked over by Joe and I as we rushed to shake his hand and seal the deal. These much more powerful engines would undoubtedly enhance the performance of our new boats once we started fishing.

Lilian and I now had a family of four children and several years previous we had purchased a large residential caravan and had it sited at Burghead so that during Easter and summer school holidays the family could spend their time closer to me and the boat. We have three boys and as they got older each in turn worked as holiday crew relief on Bahati or on our salmon fishing station. With Bahati sold I was now involved full time in the salmon fishing and living in the caravan at Burghead. One evening I returned to the caravan and found a note pushed into the edge of the doorframe. It read simply, "Please telephone this Fochabers telephone number and ask for Ben Yami". This had me completely mystified because I didn't know anyone in Fochabers and certainly knew no one with a foreign name like Ben Yami. After I had eaten I walked into the village to the telephone box and phoned this number. The lady who answered asked me to hang on while she would go and find him. A minute or so later a gentleman came to the phone and told me that he was an Israeli fishing gear technologist who was holidaying in the area and he would like to come and see our salmon fishing operation. I said that would be no problem and that I would be very happy to show him our fishing operation. We arranged that he would come to Hopeman and meet up with us on the following morning. Next morning he duly arrived at the appointed time and we set off out to sea in the salmon cobble to fish our nets. He was obviously very interested in our work and said that he'd never expedience any method of fishing even remotely similar to this before. Once we got back to the harbour and had landed and iced the fish we had caught, he accompanied me across to our net repairing yard where he was soon engaged in measuring and recording all the details of the construction of our bag nets. When lunchtime came he invited me to have lunch with him at the local pub. This invitation I was glad to accept. Once we had got a drink and sat down to lunch he started to ask questions about the new boat that I was having built. I wondered how the hell he knew about that. Then he really started to quiz me about all the details involved in the specification of the new boat. He asked when I would next be going down to the boatyard and if it might be possible for him to accompany me and see the craft under construction. I replied that as I had no pressing work commitments on the salmon station, if he wanted to, I could take him down to Buckie that afternoon. When we arrived at the boatyard I introduced him to Mr. Thompson the owner who volunteered to show Ben Yami around the yard and over the boat under construction. Mr. Thompson was subject to a barrage of questions and observations as the tour progressed. I overheard him asking Mr. Thompson at one point what in his estimation the shortest possible time would be before my boat would be ready to launch. When we were finally ready to leave he expressed his gratitude to Mr. Thompson for spending so much time with him and went on to congratulate him on the obvious quality and expertise of his workforce producing a very high standard finished boat. When we set off to return home Ben Yami suddenly began quizzing me about the work I had done in East Africa and how had I enjoyed working with Benzion Kagan, the Israeli fish-canning expert, that I had assisted during his FAO funded research program. By this time I really was in a quandary about who this guy really was and how he came to know so much about me. As if he had read my mind he then announce that he was in fact the Chief Fishing Gear Technologist of FAO and he wanted to offer me a short term post as an FAO adviser to work in the Solomon Islands in the Pacific for six months. I was completely gob smacked at this offer, but as I had been offered a post with FAO years previously, as mentioned near the start of this book, I was not going to make the same mistake twice and so I immediately accepted his offer subject to the condition that I was guaranteed to be home in time for the launch of my boat. He was quite happy to agree to this and said the paperwork would be sent to me in the next few days and I should prepare myself to set off for the Far East in the very near future. My mind was already full of palm covered islands and tropical temperatures, just the environment I was designed to live in. Even more important was the fact that I would be on an FAO salary that is tax-free and the amount of money that I would earn in six months employed by them would certainly go a long way towards meeting my full deposit required on the new boat. Lilian while envious was quite happy for me to take up this position as it would make such a big financial difference to our situation, so I immediately set about getting all my clothing and things I would need gathered together ready for my departure. Then one morning about 10 days before I was due to fly off, I received a letter from the Aberdeen Royal Infirmary informing me that I was to be admitted in one month's time for my long awaited stomach ulcer operation. To say I was devastated would be an understatement, but I had lived in pain and discomfort, swallowing countless pills, for several years rather than months. The opportunity of having the operation carried out with time to recuperate before the new boat was ready I just could not afford to turn down. I had to call Ben Yami in his FAO headquarters office in Rome to explain the situation to him and apologize for not being able to take up a post he had offered. Fortunately he was very understanding and while disappointed that I wouldn't be able to carry out the work for FAO he wished me well and a speedy recovery.

Our three sons were obviously getting older and the eldest was now bigger than me and the thought of trying to provide pocket money for them all was a daunting prospect. I had therefore decided that I would buy them a small inshore fishing boat so that they could make money for themselves in their spare time. The boat I had just bought had come from the Orkney Islands and had belonged to a lighthouse keeper there. It was a traditional Stroma yole, a very beamy and safe class of inshore boat.

The boat required some work done on it. That was the reason I had been able to afford to buy it. The hull was fine but there was a small forward wheelhouse which might have fitted very small people, but was like a straightjacket on me or any of my sons. This was the first thing that had to go. The boat's engine was an old BMC van engine that had been crudely marinised. For reliability and safety it also had to go. In the four weeks I had available before being admitted to hospital I managed to complete all the work needed, including the installation of a new 22 hp lightweight air cooled diesel engine and the complete decking of the boat. I had absolutely no concerns about giving the boat to our sons as they had all spent enough time with me on Bahati and on our salmon cobble to be more than capable of handling this small boat. I was of the opinion that working this boat and earning their own money in their spare time would instil in them that rewards were entirely dependent on their own effort, and that they would quickly find the real cost of making money.

The rebuilding work had kept me fully employed during this period and also helped to occupy my mind from dwelling on the forthcoming operation. Finally the day of admission to hospital arrived and I had to resign myself to their care. I would prefer to glass over the 10 days spent in hospital sufficient to say that I was very glad when I was allowed to go home for recuperation. Lilian had come to the hospital to pick me up and take me home in her Mini. Up until that point I had not realized just how much the operation had taken out of me. I thought that her car must be fitted with square wheels because every small bump in the road felt to me like we were going over the Grand Canyon. The next day I set off to walk the 75 yards down to the harbour.By the time I reached there I was grateful to collapse onto one of the public benches and needed about half an hour to recover enough to be able to undertake the journey home. I made steady progress with my recovery and regaining my strength and by the date for the launching of my boat I was almost fully fit. We travelled from home in Stonehaven to Buckie on the morning of the launch. When we arrived at Thompson's boat yard it was already swarming with friends and guests. We had time to chat amongst them before taking a short walk round the boat seeing it resting almost precariously on the launching cradle. We then gathered at the bow of the boat in front of the assembled guests and boat yard staff and Lilian named and launched the boat. Then after a short pause while the final props were knocked out Bahati began to move and accelerated out of the building shed and down the slides on the steeply sloping shingle beach and off out into the sea. There it was met by another fishing boat, taken under tow, guided into the harbour and moored up alongside a quay. Once there any guest that desired could go on board and walk around the boat. When every one who wanted to had been onboard the new boat, the quests all started of up the hill to a bespoke local hotel where a celebratory lunch had been laid on by Mr Thompson. After we had finished our excellent lunch accompanied with liberal amounts of alcohol it was time for the speeches. I had to lead off offering thanks to Mr Thompson and all his workforce for the work that they had so far undertaken on our boat, and suggesting I would now appreciate its early completion!. I then went on to thank the Volvo company for their generous assistance toward the cost of the improved engine installation for our boat. The other partners all expressed their appreciation of the builders and all their workers and commended the builders on the high standard of workmanship displayed at every point of the build. Mr Thompson was most impressed with our guest list. He said that he had never had so many "toffs" attending any of his previous launches. The guests included my friends Sir Alex Buchanan Smith and his wife. Alex was then the secretary of state for Scotland. We also had Sir Kenneth Alexander who at that time was the chairman of the Highland Board, but who had in the past been the chairman of Upper Clyde Shipbuilders. He was an old university and lifelong friend of Bill Dixon. Altogether we had a very enjoyable day, my main thought as we set off home was how long would we have to wait before the boat was finally completed and ready for sea. Hopefully no more than four months.

Bill Dixon's youngest son who was a recent fisheries science graduate was going to come aboard the boat as a crewman once we started fishing to help widen his experience in the commercial fishing industry. He had been working on an oyster and muscle marine farm on Loch Fyne but was keen to come home to Stonehaven. The local small boats at the time were all making a good living, weather permitting, operating traditional muscle lines and catching cod. My two elder sons had been using their boat at the weekends for this purpose and had been doing quite well. I therefore took over the boat during the week and Peter Dixon and I went baited line fishing for the first time in either of our lives. Each day we had to shell more than a bag of muscles a job, that initially seemed to take us forever until we gained expertise. We then had to bait the line of over 1500 hooks and stow it carefully into two shallow sided trays so that once the two trays were loaded with the baited line we could take them to sea and lay out the line at full speed from our boat, guiding it out over a metal funnel while ensuring that none of the hooks accidentally got snagged in other areas of the line. Initially the work seemed to be unending and we had to endure a very steep learning curve but it was proving profitable and in a relatively short time we became much more proficient.

Finally word was received that a date could be set for taking the new boat to sea and conducting her sea trials. I had been on the boat daily for the last week familiarizing myself with all the new equipment, accompanied by Joe Kemlo who was a qualified mechanic and was going to be our engineer. By the time trials day arrived we were quite sure that we had mastered all the new equipment. As is normal the senior surveyor from the White Fish Authority was to conduct the sea trials and ensure that everything to the last detail was working and met with every letter of the specification. In addition he had to test and examine all the regulation survival equipment on board along with fire fighting equipment and bilge and gas alarms. Once he was completely satisfied I was allowed to sign off the boat on behalf of the joint owners and take it to sea for a first relatively short voyage westwards along the coast to Burghead where all our fishing gear and equipment was waiting. It took us a couple of days to get all the trawl wires, trawl doors, nets and other equipment set up and ready to go to sea. The next morning we sailed from Burghead and going a few miles offshore we shot the trawl gear for the first time. We did not intend to catch any fish but merely wanted to pay out all the trawl wire and get the winches to recover the gear under the heavy load of working conditions so that the wire was wound onto the winch drums carefully while under strain. All went well and we got the trawl doors up and made fast while we attached the net to the pennants from the twin barrelled net drum that hauled our net aboard for the very first time. Having demonstrated that everything was working properly, we set sail for Stonehaven to let our families and friends see over the boat before we started going to sea for real at the beginning of the next week.

Big Bahati under construction At Thompson's of Buckie.

Me standing in the prop. space.

Bahati ready for launching.

Mc Donald and Dixon families at the launch.

My wife Lilian smashes the bottle and names Bahati.

Bahati finally enters the water.

Chapter 9.

We had no intention of starting pair trawling with
Kadana immediately. We were going to need some time
getting used to the boat before we started fishing as a
pair. Shooting and hauling up the pair gear means that the
boats have to come very close together, and we certainly
didn't want to put ourselves in the unnecessary danger of
colliding before we fully understood the capabilities of
our boats. Since Joe had taken over Kadana and started
fishing he had normally been working on the prawn
grounds about 100 miles northeast Buckie. He was
landing prawns and fish and was very pleased with his
boat but in that area he was working in deep water over
soft ground, not the type of fishing grounds we would be
working over as a pair team fishing for cod and other
white fish species. When we first put to sea with Bahati
things did not go very well. We were trawling over the
very hard inshore grounds and the gear we had purchased
for the boat just was not up to the job. The boat was
obviously producing far more bollard pull than had been
anticipated. This was largely due to the underwater shape
of the hull in conjunction with the Kort nozzle that the
boat was equipped with. We kept breaking spreader wires
and even ground chains without being able to detect from
the boat that we had snagged on something solid enough
to cause the damage. When these breakages occurred it
meant that whatever side of the net was subject to the
broken sweep, that wing of the net would fold back and
take the tension out of the net, allowing the belly of the
net to rest on the seabed and get torn to ribbons. We
seemed to be spending more time mending nets and
replacing the broken gear and sweeps than we did fishing

and certainly didn't land very much fish. We had to replace all the ground gear, both wire and chain, with much stronger replacements. We had our bollard pull tested and were very surprised to find we had a static bollard pull of just over four tons. This figure was more than 25% greater than had originally been anticipated by the naval architect on whose power estimates the purchase of our gear had been made. If you happen to be towing with the following tide, with a 25 ton boat,4 tons of bollard pull, plus a couple of knots of tide, the total power developed easily explained the amount of breakages we had been enduring. I had spoken to Bill Dixon, my partner and internationally famous fishing gear technologist. In an evening he had drawn up a detailed plan for a new trawl net. It was a four panel trawl net very different from the conventional two panel net we had been using. We took the design up to Jackson Trawls Peterhead and Arthur Jackson quickly made us up two nets. As soon as we took these nets aboard and set them up on our new much heavier ground gear things immediately changed beyond all recognition. When some of the old trawl skippers in Aberdeen saw the weight and size of our ground gear they told us in no uncertain terms that they thought we were mad because our ground gear was as heavy as the gear they had used on their much larger steel side trawlers. They had to eat their words however when, after a few weeks, we really got into our stride and started to make regular good catches. It was like chalk and cheese on board the boat as soon as we started with Bill's nets and the heavier ground gear. We could fish on the hardest of ground sometimes for a full week without damaging our net. Bahati was not fitted with a power block when she was built. Our twin three ton net drum took care of hauling the net and ground gear aboard and if you kept the boat going ahead when you heaved up on the dog rope to the cod end you got a good lift of fish to take aboard. Very frequently we would have more than one lift of fish so we had to throw away the cod end again and speed the boat up to drive the rest of the fish back down the bag and into the lifter, before heaving up on the dog rope again. This was time consuming but once again Bill came up with an answer. Bahati was fitted with a high and strong stern gantry built of box section steel. It was ten inch sided at the bottom reducing to eight inch sided at the top with an eight inch sided cross bar across the full width of the gantry. We lifted all our fish on board with this gantry with the full cod end sliding on board through the open section of our transom. Bill got our shore engineers to weld a U shaped six inch pipe onto the underside of the cross member through which we passed a dog rope with a split hook on the seaward end and the other end reaching to our winch. He then told us to attach a set of lifting rings round our bag half way down the length of the bag. The dog rope from this set of rings was hooked onto the net's headline. When we hauled up and the headline of the net came onboard we simply hooked the dog rope from the middle of our net to the dog rope through the U shaped guide on the gantry and heaved in. This ran our catch into the lifting bag of the cod end very efficiently. When we had more fish in the bag after the cod end was thrown back into the sea we just hauled the dog rope to the mid bag up again and ran the catch into the cod end. When we wanted to take the bag aboard we simply had to pull the folded bag right through the U bracket and once the cod end was aboard we slacked the dog rope back and all the bag of our net fell down to the deck safely on board no manual hauling being required at all. By now it was early October and while we were fishing quite well, periods of worsening weather were beginning to affect us.

Joe Aitkin then phoned up and told me that some pairs of Buckie steel built small stern trawlers commonly referred to as "the tin boats" were fishing in Cornwall for mackerel and were doing very well. These tin boats were virtually the same size and power as Kadana and Bahati so we decided to apply for the necessary fishing licence and get ready to set off for Cornwall. We took delivery of mackerel pair trawls for each boat and completed fitting out the boats for handling bulk catches. By the time the fishing licenses had arrived we were ready to sail. Kadana set off from Buckie and we had arranged that he would call us ashore as he approached Aberdeen. We would then set sail and link up with them and set off down the British East Coast in close company. The weather was quite kind to us and we made good time as we sailed down the coast. All went well until crossing the Thames estuary when a severe weather warning was broadcast warning of extreme south westerly gales in all sea areas along the English south coast. By the time we were approaching Dover we were feeling the full effect of these increasing gales. We had been seeing the channel ferries coming and going as we neared the port. As we neared the north entrance to Dover harbour I called up the port control to inform them we were two Scottish fishing boats approaching the north entrance to the port to shelter from the coming weather. No response was forthcoming. We had actually entered the port before the harbour control came on the radio obviously rather miffed that we had not contacted them. I responded saying that I had called him up on the designated radio channel several times a short time previous giving details of our boats and that we intended to enter the port to seek shelter from the steadily increasing gale. They couldn't very well tell us to bugger off but they certainly did not give any encouragement to stay. We were told that there were absolutely no berths available alongside any of the quays in the port. If we wanted to remain in the port we should proceed towards the South side of the harbour and anchor behind a big stone jetty that came from the beach out into the middle of the harbour. This stone jetty was certainly high enough to provid adequate shelter from the screaming wind but there was an uncomfortable jabble in the harbour due to the seas crashing over the outer breakwaters and the swell entering the south harbour entrance. We had to spend two full days anchored in this location before the weather started to moderate. This was the gale when a large dockyard crane in Plymouth or Portsmouth was blown over on top of a warship and caused major damage. Many of the small towns along the southwest coast suffered a lot of structural damage, and when we finally got to Newlyn we found that many of the roofs of the old houses in the town had been badly damaged and were covered over by tarpaulins. For a large part of our time in Dover the cross channel ferries had not been sailing. The gale finally subsided and the weather forecast was promising improving conditions so we wanted to set off for the southwest. We were however short of milk and bread and some other stores so we contacted port control requesting permission to go along side somewhere so that we could go into town and make these purchases. From the response I think they thought we wanted to land on the moon. However, after much discussion, we were told to approach and go behind the ferry terminals into a nicely sheltered small harbour with yards and yards of empty quayside. There was absolutely no reason on earth why we couldn't have been tied up in this sheltered small harbour for the past two days instead of being anchored off, except for the bloody mindedness of some jumped up minor port official. We were no sooner tied up alongside when the f***king immigration officers arrived wanting to know what part of the world we come from. The names of Bahati and Kadana were possibly confusing for them but I asked them if they were familiar with the British fishing boat registration system and if our registration numbers were not big and bold enough to give them a clue. They left apparently satisfied. We then managed to get a taxi and the two cooks went up into town and bought the necessary supplies. As soon as they returned we cast off and set off through the south entrance of this inhospitable loony bin of a port and buffeted our way westwards through the not inconsiderable swell that was still running after the severe gales. We sailed on past the Isle of Wight then just as we were approaching Portland Bill Joe came on the radio and informed me that he was getting dangerously low on fuel as he had sailed eight hours more than us. After looking at the chart we decided that Weymouth was the closest and probably the biggest and best harbour to make for. After we entered the harbour and tied up the harbour master arrived wanting to know how we were going to pay our harbour dues. Everywhere in Scotland when you enter a harbour you simply tell them the name of your fish selling company and that's the end of story. In England it was obviously very different. You had to produce credit cards or authorized bank drafts before any service would be provided. We inquired about getting fuel and were told that the only fuel that was available in the port came from a small floating fuel barge equipped with a diesel pump like a garage fore court. It finally came alongside and inquired about how much fuel we wanted, and when Joe said we would probably take 1000 gallons in each boat the fuel supplier almost past away. When he had recovered sufficiently he informed us that he would only be able to supply us with about 200 gallons on each boat as that was all the fuel he had. Before he would even start to put any fuel into the boats he demanded payment. Cash had to be transferred from our fish salesmen's offices in Scotland to his local bank before he would supply the fuel. We wondered just what the hell sort of uncivilized country we had come to and whether it was going to be as bad at any other port that we entered. The small amount of fuel we had taken on board was only going to be enough to see us to Brixham harbour, that we understood to be a major English Fishing port. When they finally entered the harbour there we were not overly impressed and when we inquired about getting fuel we were told that we would have to wait as a small tanker was delivering fuel to the oil base and we would not be able to get any fuel until its delivery was complete and it had cleared the berth. When we finally got alongside the fuel berth there was still a lot of hassle about means of payment but it was not quite as bad as the last two ports. As soon as we were fuelled up we set off once more on our way to the west. After passing to seaward of first Start Point and then Prawl point where we set our course for The Lizard which would mark the entrance to Mounts Bay and our destination of Newlyn. As soon as we entered Newlyn harbour we began to feel that it was more like home. Here there were genuine fishermen and fishing boats being catered for efficiently by the shore-based organizations. We became part of the small fleet of Scottish pocket trawlers that were working out of the harbours of Newlyn and Penzance. We got all the details about what the boats in the fleet were allowed to catch and where they were currently working. There was a strict quota in place governing how much mackerel you could land in any week. The other boats in the fleet had found that dependent on weather you could catch two weeks quota in eight days fishing time. If you arrived back onboard your boats on a Tuesday night you could be sure of catching that week's quota by the Saturday. From Sunday to Wednesday you caught the following week's quota, allowing you to drive home to Scotland over night on the Wednesday night then returning overnight to Cornwall on the following Tuesday night to be ready for sea on the Wednesday morning. Unfortunately most of the catches from the inshore fleet were destined to go for reduction to meal and oil as the many big refrigerated stern trawlers and purse seiners with refrigerated brine tanks commanded virtually all the human consumption markets.

Right from the start we managed to catch our quotas but to begin with it took us a lot more fishing time than the other members of the fleet. However after a few weeks we were as efficient as any of the other boats in our class. On the day before setting off home for the Christmas break we had been fishing on the east side of the Lizard off the entrance to Falmouth. We were fishing this far east because there was a heavy swell running in Mounts Bay. By lunchtime we had our quota of about 30 tons of mackerel in each boat and because of the heavy swell in Mounts Bay we called ashore to our Newlyn agents to see if we could land our catches in Falmouth and leave our boats there for the Christmas break. Unfortunately we were told this was impossible because all the outlets there were already contracted to take their total capacity from the large boats that were waiting their turn to discharge. There was nothing for it but to set off back for Penzance despite the heavy swell. This meant sailing round the Lizard once more before we could ease ourselves onto a north westerly course up towards Newlyn and Penzance. There was very little wind and it was only the height of the Atlantic swell that was of concern. There is a famous tide race off the Lizard and the Admiralty charts and handbooks caution you that you must keep well offshore or very close inshore to avoid the worst of sea conditions as you sail past this point. As we approached this area with a strong following tide I thought that I had gone far enough out to sea, and indeed a coaster of about 2000 tons was catching us up quickly and was on a course to pass us close on our seaward side. We then began to feel the effects of the tide race and from nowhere the swells became almost mountainous and they were unbelievably steep and close together. I was standing behind the wheel but I had to bend my knees right down to be able to see the top of the oncoming wave through the wheelhouse windows and then when it reached us it felt like we were going up in a lift until we reached the waves summit. At this point from our forward wheelhouse it appeared that we were about to go over a cliff as we sailed down the slope to the bottom of the valley between the waves, only to repeat the thrills and anxieties as we roller coasted over each successive wave. It was at this point that the coaster overtook us sailing about 150 yards off on our port side. I just could not believe what I was seeing as on at least two occasions I saw completely underneath the hull of the ship because the length of the ship meant that he was straddling several waves and so he wasn't going violently up-and-down like us. As soon as we passed through the tide race the sea state rapidly returned to normal and the heavy swell was not in the least bit threatening. We then altered course for Penzance. Once through the lock gates there and into the sheltered basin we discharged our catches and securely tie up our boats for the Christmas break while we went home to Scotland. On the long road trips up and down from Penzance to Aberdeen I usually drove our crew's car while our engineer, Joe Kemlo, drove the Kadana's car. We tended to drive faster than anybody else and the crews were happy to put their lives in our hands. At that time it was 714 miles by road from Penzance to Aberdeen and we usually completed this journey in just under 11 hours. This included two stops for meals and refuelling the two cars. These stops were normally made at a service station near Exeter and then at the service station near Lanark when travelling north, or Carlisle and Exeter when returning south. Joe Aitken normally drove their car for the last 70 miles from Stonehaven to their homes in Buckie. We never experienced any problems on any of our high-speed journeys during our time fishing in Cornwall.

We set off back to Cornwall on the morning of 4 January but when we reached Newlyn later that night we were met with a disaster. The other Buckie trawlers had set off from home the previous evening and had gone to sea as soon as they arrived at Penzance. One of the Buckie pair teams, Bounteous and Loranthus, had been fishing fairly close to shore on the west side of Newlyn and they had just made one big haul of mackerel and the Bounteous had the haul of fish hanging from its after gallows. Suddenly without any prior warning the boat listed and then rolled over and sank. The Loranthus was lying only a few yard away and managed to rescue the three crewmen who surfaced but the boat's skipper and two other crew men had lost their lives. Lifeboats and emergency services were still at the scene but everyone knew that there was no hope for any of the missing men. We went aboard our boats to make sure everything was in order after the long Christmas break and then had something to eat and a few hours sleep before we set off back up to Scotland. A Cornish commercial diving team quickly salvage the sunken boat and recovered the bodies of the three missing crewmen. We were able to attend their funerals at Buckie about a week later. When we returned to Cornwall after the funerals our hearts and minds somehow didn't seem to be on our continuing work in that location. We only continued to fish there for a couple of weeks before we decided we had had enough and set off to sail home, up the West Coast this time using the Caledonian canal as the route back to the Scottish East Coast. On one of our last days fishing in Cornwall we made a very welcome but unexpected catch. We were fishing in daylight and mackerel shoals were moving very fast not only horizontally but vertically in the water as well. Watching on our sonar and echo sounders we were trying to keep our nets vertically in line with the fast moving shoals while at the same time watching the display from the sounder on the headline of the trawl to monitor any fish entering the net. I only noted that an unusual succession of larger single fish were entering the net but no evidence of any shoals of mackerel so we presumed we had missed them, and hauled up. Once the net reached the surfaced it was obvious that there were some fish in the net making a lot of splashing and when we hauled the bag up to the boat we discover that we had caught a good haul of large sea bass. Once they were all on board and boxed we discovered that we had 93 boxes of these relatively expensive fish and when we landed them at Newlyn they sold for just over ten thousand five hundred pounds which made a nice going away present as we departed Cornwall.

After we had rounded Lands End we set a course to clear Ramsey island at the north end of St. Brides Bay. Having passed this island and shortly after passing St David's Head, Joe Aitken called me up from Kadana to say that they had picked something up into their propeller and that we would have to take them under tow. Having turned our boat round and sailed back towards them, we picked up the end of his towrope, made it fast, and set off with Kadana under tow. I scrutinized the chart and thought that Fishguard was probably the best port to make for. Fishguard we understood was an important ferry terminal connecting Wales and Ireland. As we approached the pier heads in the pitch black in the middle of the night we were definitely underwhelmed with what we saw. We were confused by what appeared to be a major obstruction lying across most of the harbour entrance. Repeated radio calls to a supposed port control office went unanswered. We had no option but pass slowly between the obstruction and the breakwater and head onwards into the harbour to where the charts said the quayside was. As we neared this point we saw that there was one ship lying against the quay. It was a Navy boom defence ship. I manoeuvred our boat alongside Kadana and with both boats lashed side-by-side I jockeyed our boats alongside the navy ship. A night watchman then appeared on the ship and took our mooring ropes and we made our boats secure alongside. Ashore there appeared to be absolutely nothing going on, no sign of human life or traffic of any description, and we the aliens from distant lands had just landed. The watchman could tell us nothing but said the crew would be aboard before 7am and they might be able to give us some information. Nothing for it, we went to bed for a few hours sleep then just before 7am a Scottish voice was calling us to see if anybody was awake. This voice turned out to be from the captain of the navy craft. We explained our situation to him and asked if there were any commercial diving firms in the area that we could contact, who could dive down to Kadan's sterngear and cut away the obstruction. He then said that he had a diving team aboard his ship and while they were not really supposed to, he felt sure they would help us. He went off to speak with them and shortly returned telling us that they were getting into their diving gear. He came into our mess deck and sat down for some breakfast with us. By his voice he obviously came from the Fife area of Scotland. He asked me if I knew the KY Nimrod, a boat of similar size to ours from Anstruther. I said I did know the boat and her skipper and frequently worked close by them. He went on to tell me that he was a brother of the Nimrod's skipper. His diving team quickly cleared Kadana's stern gear of the ropes and an old hatch cover that were jammed into his Kort nozzle stopping the propeller. They did not want to take any payment but we persuaded them to take at least enough to buy themselves a drink on us. I asked him about the obstruction in the harbour entrance and apparently it was the hulk of a burnt out Irish cattle transporter that had sunk there but had not as yet being salvaged. With both boats operational again we said our farewells and set of once more on our homeward journey. Thankfully there were no further incidents before we passed through the Caledonian Canal and reached our home waters of the North Sea.

Buckie boat collects Bahati to tow her into Buckie.

Bahati alongside the fish market in Buckie.

Wheel house looking forward.

Wheelhouse looking aft.

The Galley and mess deck.

Showing part of the six man cabin.

Chapter 10.

On our return from Cornwall we went home to Stonehaven with Bahati to unload all our pelagic nets and equipment and deposit them all in our store there. We then had to sail up to Aberdeen with the boat to pickup our trawl doors, nets and other whitefish handling equipment. In addition we took on board nearly three hundred empty fish boxes and ten tons of ice. With our fuel and water tanks topped up we were ready for sea. When we resumed fishing it was almost the "hungry month of March."

Our fishing gear was now working very well but it was still very difficult at this time of year to do more than keep trying to ensure that all the crew had a living wage each week. It was particularly hard if you had disruptive spells of bad weather because on Scottish fishing boats all the crew work on a share basis. This means that all the boat's expenses every week have to be paid and this cost is taken from the gross sales figure. At that time our expenses were regularly between £700 and £1000 pounds a week depending mainly on fuel costs and landing charges. Even if we didn't go to sea due to bad weather we still had a minimum weekly cost of about £500 pounds to pay. This was the cost of boat insurance, crew insurance, harbour dues and hire charges for electronic and navigational equipment. After all these expenses had been taken off the gross sales the net figure was divided into two. One half went to the owners of the boat and the fishing gear, while the other half was divided equally amongst all members of the crew so that everyone from cook to skipper received the same working wage. On some boats the skipper took a the very small percentage more than the rest of the crew because of the responsibility he was carrying, but I personally never did this, I liked to keep the system with everybody sharing equally. One of the beauties of this system is that the skipper seldom if ever has to say anything to any of the crew members if he thinks that someone is not pulling their weight. The other crew members quickly make their feelings known to any slacker in no uncertain terms and any failing crewman either bucks up his ideas or he leaves the boat of his own accord and looks for another job. The half of the net figure that goes to the owners has to pay for all maintenance and replacement costs on the boat and fishing gear as well as meeting the considerable repayment of loan and interest charges on the capital cost of the boat. This all means that if you don't get to sea for a week you have to pay two or more weeks' expenses before the crew start making any wages. The pressure of all these economic facts weigh heavily on the skipper. He has to decide when it is possible and safe to go to sea as the weather improves, as well as deciding when he has to stop fishing as the weather deteriorates. These decisions are made in the knowledge that the safety of his crew is his responsibility combined with the fact that the decisions he makes affects his crew's earnings as well as his own. The financial situation of six families depends on the decisions he makes. I have sometimes found myself going to sea after an extended spell of bad weather facing the fact that I would have to catch more than five thousand pounds worth of fish before we as a crew started to make a penny. The skipper's situation in those days was hard enough but what it must feel like to be a skipper in the present day with all the quota restrictions, limited days at sea, and other legal restrictions that they are faced with, I think could well go a long way to explaining the number of men and boats being lost at sea.

We fished as a single boat until well into June when finally Joe Aitken said he wanted to try out our initial plan of pair trawling. We put all our single boat trawl gear into the store in Aberdeen and took on board the large white fish pair trawl along with a fifty fathom heavy trawl warp single sweep. This sweep would be subject to the maximum amount of abrasion on the seabed travelling immediately in front of the net spreaders as we dragged our gear. When you are engaged in single boat bottom trawling you normally pay out three times the depth of water as the length of wire required between the boat and your trawl doors. In pair trawling you would normally use at least twice if not as much as three times that length of wire, plus the fifty fathoms of much heavier trawl warp immediately in front of the net. Once you had shot your net and your partner boat was securely connected to his side of the net you each paid out the required length of wire and started towing. We would normally be towing the gear with the boats maintaining a constant quarter of a mile between the boats. It may be necessary to change the length of the wires during the course of a tow if we found ourselves in deeper water. To maintain the maximum efficiency in shepherding any fish into the path of the net you had to try and keep a minimum of 100 fathoms of wire in contact with the seabed. We normally operated a system where one skipper would in effect be controlling the path of the two boats during the course of the tow. Providing your decks were cleared of fish this gave the other skipper a chance to go below and get a couple of hours sleep. We normally tried to tow for a minimum of four hours provided we didn't come fast on the seabed. Then it was a case of all hands on deck as we started to heave up. You try to maintain a parallel course gradually converging towards each other as you haul up until all the trawl wire and the single sweep is on the winch and only the net spreaders and net remain in the sea. A heaving line is then thrown from one boat to the other and the wire pennant from whichever boat is going to haul the net is passed across and attached to the end of the spreaders. Once this has been accomplished the boat that is not involved in hauling the net lets the spreaders go and the hauling boat then starts hauling up with the net drum until all the net is onboard as far as the centre of the ground gear. Any catch is now visible on the surface in the bag. The other boat will go alongside the cod end and dependent on how much fish there is in the bag will take up to three lifts of fish on board. This was as much fish as we had working deck space for in either of our boats. If there was more fish in the net the other boat then lifted them aboard. And the whole procedure of shooting the net could commence again.

When we first went to sea with Kadana I could not say that we did not have a fair share of teething problems. Neither Joe nor I were particularly familiar with these offshore fishing grounds and while we did have knowledge of the position of wrecks and other main obstructions we were not overly familiar in the early weeks with varying contours of the seabed we were working over. Because of our inexperience we became fast to the seabed quite frequently and there was substantial damage to the net that then had to be repaired on board, while the net from the other boat was shot and the tow resumed. When I had designed the deck layout of my boat I had the boat built with an opening in the transom on the port side from deck level so that the net could be hauled up and along the deck by the net drum. I had sited my net drum as far forward as possible. This meant that I could wind on the net and leave all the centre of the net that was subject to most damage readily available spread out on the deck for repair. In the case of Kadana however there was no stern opening and Joe had his net drum positioned under the stern gantry quite close to the stern rail. This was possibly ideal for working in the deep offshore waters where he normally worked for prawns and fish. There he would expect very little net damage. It was far from ideal however for pair trawling over hard ground because if the heavy net had been wound on to the drum to get it over the boat's transom and onboard and it was found to be badly damaged, it had to be manually hauled off the net drum and forward onto the working deck to get enough clear space to repair it. Despite the problems, we did manage to make some good catches and our burden of problems gradually diminished as our experience of the grounds grew. We were both horrified however by the amount of undersized fish or discards that we were regularly catching in every haul. The bags in both our nets were well above the minimum mesh size but once the weight of fish started to build up in the cod end it was very obvious that nothing was escaping through the mesh of the bag because of the strain that each mesh was under. We did not think that this would auger well for the future of our fish stocks if pair trawling became more widely adopted by the fleet unless some modification of the gear could be devised to allow more fish to escape and survive. In late summer Kadana had been booked for the slip for its annual overhaul and paint and we had been booked for the slip almost immediately after he was to come off. This was going to mean that we would be a full month without being able to pair trawl so Joe decided that he would just put his single boat gear back on board and go back to deep water fishing for prawns and fish. We in turn had to put our fishing gear ashore before going to the slip for our annual refit so we also consigned our pair trawl to the store ready to resume single boat working once off the slip. We resumed our single boat working and managed to make a reasonable living right through the winter and into the following spring.

Probably due to my television appearances as a spokesman for the various sectors of the fishing industry on the seals issue and my much publicised work on the mesh size debate in the sprat fishery, I found myself getting involved in fisheries politics. I became a member of the Scottish Fishermen's Federation and before too long found myself being appointed as chairman of the Aberdeen branch of the Fishermen's Federation and shortly after that I became a director of the Federation. That wasn't something that I had any particular desire to get involved in. It was increasingly obvious that life for fishermen was going to become increasingly difficult due to measures being pushed by both the British and European Parliaments. As nobody fights harder than a person who is directly affected, I thought it best that I should become involved in all matters that were particularly going to affect my sector of the fishing industry. I soon found myself a regular visitor to the government marine research laboratory in Aberdeen and meeting with the men who were conducting the research programs that were likely to have a relevance to future legislation. There were may concerns being raised by fishermen about the number and ever increasing size and power of new boats coming into service. The fish stocks, the scientists were advising us, were becoming increasingly under pressure of overfishing but we were finding it impossible to get the government to initiate any action. The fishermen's organizations were trying to persuade the government that some form of licensing had to be brought in to control the size of the fleet. Each current owner of a registered vessel should get a licence automatically but any future licences should only be issued if a similar catching capacity in the fleet had been decommissioned. We were recommending to the government that the licence must always remain the property of the government so that licences wouldn't begin to have any financial value to the licence holder. If they were the property of the government they could be withdrawn for fixed periods as a penalty for any breach of fishing regulations. We tried our best to explain to the government that the licence must have a relationship to the catching capacity of the boat licensed. This would prevent boats with a licence being replaced by a new supposedly replacement boat that had multiples of the catching capacity of the boat originally licensed. The government assured us that we need not concern ourselves on this issue as they would closely monitor the situation and would not allow it to cause any problems!!! Too late!! The government did nothing positive about the licensing program. The paper licence owners of old done and useless boats with engines of sixty to ninety HP were selling these old boats complete with licence for many multiples of the boat's worth. These boats were then scrapped and replaced in many cases with a new boat partially financed by the British government, along with up to a twenty five percent grant from the EU. In many cases the replacement boats were over eighty feet in length with eight hundred +HP engines. Any blind person with a glass marble pushed up their arse for an eye could see that this would end in disaster. I can only assume that the idiot bureaucrats that we met with in White Hall were still monitoring the situation. In a very short time the inevitable crisis we had warned of came about, and it was decided that the fleet had to be cut. Nearly fifty % of the Scottish fleet up to the present time have had to be decommissioned and scrapped out of existence. That is more than 400 boats lost from the Scottish fleet. In many cases these were the very same boats that the government and EU had helped to finance at the cost of many millions to the taxpayers.

Long before the boat licensing issue came to the fore I was present at a meeting in London with the men from the ministry. We were told that they were about to announce a complete cessation on fishing for haddock until the following year. In my innocent mind I could never understand why you had to have industrial confrontation and strikes. I thought any reasonable men should be able to discuss any situation and come to a reasoned conclusion satisfactory to all. However the men from the ministry were completely incapable of understanding that you couldn't hang a notice on a fishing net telling the haddock that haddock were prohibited from entering this net. By lunchtime I was so frustrated by their attitude that I could easily have climbed across the table and physically tried to knock some understanding into their heads. Around 60% of all fish caught in the North Sea by the Scottish fleet were haddock. If the fishermen were not to be allowed to land this species it meant that they would have to stay at sea longer and make more hauls to catch enough fish of the other species to make a commercial landing. This in turn meant that multiples of the original amount of haddock that would have been caught would end up dead entirely due to the adoption of this wasteful legislation. This was being done in the name of conservation. The fact that the reverse was about to take place mattered not to the men from the ministry. As long as their numbers in the columns in their books balanced up, in their blinkered eyes, it meant they were conserving our haddock stock.

In the May of the following year while unloading our trawl net and ground gear at Stonehaven harbour a tragic accident occurred that resulted in one of my longest serving crewmembers, Blondie Craig, being blinded. We had gone into the harbour at high tide so that the deck of the boat would be virtually level with the quayside. We had secured the stern of the boat against the quay and manually hauled the bag ashore. I then gave one of our crew a lightweight alloy block and asked him to shackle it to one of a number of metal rings on the breakwater wall immediately opposite where we were moored. I had particularly asked him to make sure it was a good ring he used as I knew that some of these rings had been damaged by earlier users. We then shackled the end of a rope to the centre of the ground gear and lead it through the block at the wall back to the winch on the boat. This meant that there would be a triangle of possible danger if anything went wrong. The weakest link in the system was the quarter inch shackle attaching the rope to the ground gear. If it broke the tail of the rope would whip back against the wall of the breakwater and could do no physical harm. The men were warned not to enter this triangle of forces at any time during the haul. We then lifted the ground gear up with the lifting tackle on the stern gantry. Once the gear was clear of the deck we started to heave it ashore with the rope to the boat's winch while simultaneously paying out the lifting tackle to allow the gear to be transferred to the surface of the quay. Then for some unexplained reason Blondie decided to go to the other side of the strain triangle. At that chance second the over-one-inch-thick ring on the wall broke and the light weight block flew towards the boat. By a million to one chance it passed over the bridge of Blondie's nose without knocking him unconscious, but the edge of the block had flown across both of his eyes blinding him instantly. Emergency services were called immediately and in less than five minutes the doctor had arrived and gave what treatment he could before Blondie was taken off to Aberdeen Royal infirmary for emergency surgery. I had of course called the police, and health and safety executive, as soon as was possible. Both services examined the location and the prevailing situation and took the usual witness statements etc. I was charged by the health and safety department with failing to provide a safe place of work but after hearing all the evidence, coupled with the evidence from an expert witness retained by the boat's insurance company, I was found not guilty. The ring on the harbour which everybody thought was steel was in fact made of cast iron. Apparently this material becomes brittle with age and if it is used on any fixtures or fittings on a harbour it has to be annealed with heat at very precise intervals to maintain its strength. The use of cast iron and necessary annealing requirements are covered by the docks and harbours regulations, but these rings had never been touched from the time of installation in the early nineteen forties. The judge at the case decided that the boats insurers and the owners of the harbour should be held jointly responsible for damages payments to Blondie. They were each to pay £250,000 pounds. Our insurers paid up immediately but Grampian regional council, the owners of the harbour, tried to avoid payment for many months and the case finally was scheduled for the high court in Edinburgh. On the morning of the case in Edinburgh all the witnesses and experts were gathered at the court lobby outside the chamber when it was announced that the council had now admitted to the joint liability. Our boats insurance company representative told me that with their legal costs the council must have almost doubled their costs by their actions, but their legal people must have had a field day.

Chapter 11.

I have mentioned in the previous chapter the grave concerns that many fishermen felt about the unavoidable slaughter of immature fish that was taking place in all areas. In earlier years boats were fitted with smaller engines and the lower horsepower meant lower stress on the nets and fish were able to escape even though the nets were traditionally constructed on the diamond mesh principle. Traditionally all mobile nets had been constructed in this fashion of diamond mesh configuration to ensure that each leg of a mesh was carrying an equal loading of the strain. Advances in net design meant that the nets became more streamlined and more efficient and allowed even greater towing speeds. Nowadays with the much bigger horsepower and higher towing speeds, regardless of the size of the mesh, once there is any bulk of fish in the net the drag on the meshes increases and all the meshes in the bag of the net take up the loading of the weight and closed up almost completely and practically no fish can escape in these conditions. Any fish that do manage to escape through the net are so badly crushed and scaled that chances of survival are minimal. In the case of Bahati and Smallwood both our nets were well above the minimum size mesh. On one occasion we were boarded and inspected by a boarding party from the fisheries protection ship HMS Leeds Castle to check our catch and also to measure our nets. Their normal net gauge for this section of the north sea simply fell through our nets and so they had to go back to their ship to get a larger sized gauge. They found and recorded that our nets and cod end were 110mm at that time the legal minimum mesh size had just been increased to 90mm. As an illustration of just how inefficient diamond mesh size is as a means of conservation, I can give the following illustration. We were working on the Turbot Bank about 50 miles east of Aberdeen. We had completed what is known as the morning haul. This means we had been towing through the darkness and hauled up the net just about an hour after dawn. As usual there was a large bulk of fish in the net when we got it to the surface. Each boat took three lifts of fish on board immediately which was as much fish as our working decks could hold. The rest of the catch was left in the bag of the net floating alongside until such time as we cleared the decks and stowed and iced the catch below. On that particular morning we took on board a total of 18 lifts of fish, nine lifts on each boat. The lifters on the cod ends of our nets normally took on board forty-five boxes of fish in every lift, which meant that between the two boats we had taken on board more than 800 boxes of fish. But when we finally finished clearing the decks of fish at around lunchtime, it was found that we had only stowed away just over 250 boxes of marketable fish between the two boats. The other 550 boxes of immature fish had been shovelled back into the sea dead, only feeding the seabirds. This level of catching and discarding was a daily ongoing process. The daylight haul in the morning was normally the biggest bulk of fish caught on any day. The biggest volume of fish with a high percentage of discards that we have experienced was 23 lifts. These hauls were all being made with nets that were well over the legal minimum mesh size and just go to prove how totally ineffective diamond mesh size regulations were in conserving fish stocks in practice. I had frequently drawn the attention of the Department of Agriculture and Fisheries senior fisheries officers to the scale of this problem but while aware of it what could they do?. You should remember that Smallwood and Bahati were relatively small boats with only 600 hp between them. We frequently found ourselves working alongside much larger pair teams with boats in excess of 80 feet in length and fitted with 750+ horsepower in each boat. Just how much of a slaughter were these vessels responsible for! I had spoken to Basil Parrish the director at that time of the Governments Marine research laboratory in Aberdeen and expressed our concerns over this problem. He informed me that he had a team of scientists working on this serious problem and he personally was seriously concerned on the issue.

In September 1981 one of the most junior fishing gear research scientists, Jack Robertson, was onboard the small research boat, Goldseeker, in Spey bay conducting a set of experiments on immature fish escaping from nets and recording the results on film by using a remote controlled underwater movie camera. He had completed his closely defined set of projects and had some sea time still available to him before the department's research boat was due to return to Buckie harbour. He decided to try something he had been thinking about for some time. He quickly cut a panel of net on the square and attached it into a prepared space he had cut in the top sheet of the trial net. By making this panel with the mesh cut on the square it meant that only the two side legs of any mesh was taking the towing strain while the two cross legs of any mesh bore little or no strain and allowed the mesh to remain open. They had time to make one trial haul observing and recording the result with the under water camera. What they witnessed was nothing short of spectacular. All the immature fish entering the net were escaping out through the square panel like a rain shower while only the occasional small fish was seen to be escaping out through the normal diamond mesh in the rest of the net. Jack Robertson was very excited with what he had seen and wanted to let his superior departmental members of staff see for themselves what he had achieved as soon as possible. He was told in no uncertain terms that what he had done was not part of his remit and that in future, if he was to have a future, he had better confine himself to carrying out the program of work set out for him. By good fortune another rather more senior member of the research staff in a different department heard from a crewman on the research boat about the remarkable short film of the square mesh trial and the escaping young fish. He demanded to see the film when he returned to the lab and immediately after seeing it took it to show to Basil Parrish the laboratory director. He in turn was so impressed that he immediately and without precedent allocated £20,000 from existing funds to allow for the immediate charter of a commercial fishing boat to carry out a necessary further research voyage. He also gave Jack Robertson total freedom to carry out this more comprehensive development work and trials on his original idea.

The first research charter was undertaken at Fraserburgh on board the FR Harvest Reaper, skipper James May. Many different sizes of square mesh panels were inserted in different positions in the top sheet ,the extension section, and cod ends of the net. These were all tried and underwater observations made and recorded. During the charter all fish caught in the diamond mesh and square mesh trials were boxed separately. They were then exposed for sale on the Fraserburgh fish market and the crew were told not to explain the different lots of catch. It is recorded in the print-up of this charter that the fish from the square mesh net brought better prices than the fish from the diamond mesh in every instance. These trials were taken back to laboratory where the information gained was worked up and final results and analysis produced, all supported by the accompanying live film evidence. It was very convincing stuff, but the senior scientists who had tried initially to suppress the square mesh idea were very scathing and as unconstructive as possible. Were it not for the enthusiasm and support from then Director Basil Parrish the plug could well have been pulled on the entire program. There were undoubtedly relatively minor problems that had to be overcome such as knot slippage when the mesh are turned to be load bearing on the square but these problems could easily be overcome by heat sealing the knots while the netting is being produced or by using woven knotless netting that can take strain in any direction. The undeniable improvement in the ability of these nets to release immature fish was plain for all to see. Basil Parrish included a continuing research and development program into the development of square mesh technology in his financial budget for the coming year. Despite the internal opposing pressures being applied by some senior staff within the department Jack Robertson carried on with his development work. It was steadily refined until it reached the point where a commercial boat could be chartered to do some direct comparative tests between using the net with square panels and using the normal commercial diamond mesh net. Some of these tests were carried out on the Heather Sprig from Buckie, a very successful prawn and whitefish boat. The huge reduction in the volume of discards in their catches was immediately evident. This greatly reduced the amount of hard and laborious labour the crew had to undertake and was therefore an immediate hit with them. It was so much of a success that the crew didn't want to use a conventional net again, but they had to use the two nets alternately to get the comparability results from the two types of net that were required. As well as the huge reduction in discards it was found that there was a great reduction in the amount of damage caused to the valuable prawns in the catch. This was because they were subject to greatly reduced compression while being towed and lifted in the cod end. The benefits of the square mesh panels were becoming evident to all but the very select opposition group of egg-heads within the laboratory.

Jack Robertson managed to raise the interest of John Main, a senior scientist in the lab, who specialized in underwater film technology and the survivability of escaping immature fish. John Main then undertook a charter at Gairloch on the west coast and recorded a lot of film on the escapement of fish through both diamond and square mesh. He then enclosed each test net in a balloon like, fine mesh outer bag fitted over the bag of the net, to enable him to capture the immature fish that had escaped through the net. These fish were then released into fish cages on the sea bed to test their survivability. All the immature fish that had forced their way out through the diamond mesh on a conventional net were found to die within two days of being released into the cage due to the pressure injuries and scaling they had been subject to. The immature fish escaping from the square mesh were all still living a couple of weeks later when they were released. If these results were not enough to get some sort of legislation introduced to allow the introduction of square mesh panels, just what was going to be required?. The dinosaur group within the lab refused to believe that this could be anything but a freak result. John Main had also discovered and recorded film showing that haddock as they become exhausted in the mouth of a net invariably swim upward in an attempt escape. This same opposition group of senior life long laboratory confined experts who had tried to repress Jack Robertson's work on square mesh now tried to dismiss these findings by saying it was the good visibility in relatively shallow water in day light that was causing this, in their eyes, abnormal behaviour. John Main then on his next charter went on to repeat the same experiment at night in the dark using underwater lighting, but he also recorded the repeated experiment using infrared technology which the fish could not detect. In every case the new fish behaviour pattern that he had discovered was seen to be replicated. The same group of diehards in the lab still tried to place doubts on his results. These new fish behaviour findings resulted in John Main inventing and perfecting a separator trawl that became widely accepted by the commercial industry.

By the mid nineteen eighties other nations around the world were beginning to take an interest in the square mesh technology that they had heard of being developed in Aberdeen. Many of these countries carried out their own further development work which in many cases led to decisions to proceed with legislation to introduce its use. Canada and the east coast of the United States, Iceland, Norway and even Australia have all introduced legislation covering the use of square mesh panels in specific fisheries that had serious discard problems. In the UK where it had all started and where it was desperately needed if we were to try to improve our fish stock, it was still considered by some in authority to be completely unproven. Jack Robertson doggedly continued on with his research however and conducted some voyages using commercial fishing boats that were deploying the twin trawl system of fishing. In this system of operation the fishing boat deploys twin identical nets between the trawl doors but with a third trawl wire connected to a heavyweight that is attached to the ends of the sweeps between the two nets in the centre of the rig. Jack Robertson then modified one of these nets by the insertion of square mesh panels in the top sheet of the bag and cod end. The catch results of every haul undertaken were closely monitored and recorded and in every case it showed that the net with the square mesh panels provided consistently superior results as compared to the unmodified net. There were vastly fewer discards in the catch and the quality of the catch gutted and stowed was markedly superior. After all the evidence had been recorded and written up the blinkered opposition group still had the temerity to suggest that the results could all be down to chance and it only reflected the composition of the fish stock that had been in front of each net.

Some of the fraction of "unconvinced scientists" set up a program of experiments to prove that diamond mesh could allow more fish to escape If it were not such a tragic waste of effort and funds it would be side splitting comedy. They started off by using a net with a very steep taper in the construction of the bag. This in its self would have rendered the net none commercial as a net constructed like this will not sweep any fish into the bag. To compound their mistakes they then shortened the length of the bag of the net to a point where it would have been impossible to work with in the real world. They then set up fishing trials and the skipper of the charter boat was told to slow his normal towing speed by one and a half knots and no research tow undertaken was to be more than one hour in duration. They caught very little fish but fish were observed escaping from the net. The test results were published however with the results that they produced being only a little inferior to the results from the square mesh trials. These results were completely invalid and artificially contrived. The scientists had started off with an end goal in mind and enforced totally unreasonable restrictions on all aspects of the trial tows made. Had the charter boat skipper been allowed to tow at the normal commercial towing speed, as had been the case in all Jack Robertson's research work, an entirely different set of results would have appeared. Also, had the tows been of the duration of four hours or more accepted as normal in the real world, and had a heavy and increasing weight and drag been applied to the cod end, every interested person at a glance would have seen that the ill-conceived research was a complete sham and all published results were invalid and artificially contrived.

All Jack Robertson's research had shown that an eighty mm square mesh size would allow virtually all immature and undersize haddock and whiting to escape. In the early nineteen nineties the British government finally introduced legislation to make legal the use of eighty mm square mesh to allow the escape of undersize fish in prawn trawls. At that time the prawn trawl had a seventy mm legal minimum mesh size. This was at least a start. Some considerable time later the government said that ninety mm square mesh would be permitted on most other whitefish nets. We already knew from Jack Robertson's trials that eighty mm square mesh allowed virtually all-undersize fish to escape. If anybody was foolish enough to try using a ninety mm square mesh bag and cod end they would have found that they caught almost no whiting and only about fifteen percent of their current haddock catch. How the hell was any fisherman supposed to operate with a limitation like that in the real world ?? No wonder no skippers showed any interest in going down the square mesh road in these circumstances and so to this day huge masses of immature fish continue to be slaughtered in nets with ever increasing minimum mesh sizes being introduced with an absolute minimum of effect.

While on this continuing rant about the failings of government scientific advisers I would now like to turn to the subject of annual fish stock assessment calculations. The EEC decided that countries round the North Sea fish pond would annually on the same date and in the same geographic position and with all the various nationalities' research boats using the same type of net, conduct fixed duration hauls each year. All the information of the recorded catches were then fed into a computer which comes up with what is supposed to be a reliable stock assessment of the north sea. The scientists then come up with maximum catch recommendations affecting all fishermen.

I think that the people who decided to select the positions that the fishing trials were to be carried out at must have thrown darts in a random fashion at a large map. Many of the areas selected were known by fishermen to never have any commercial quantities of fish present. Many more of the selected areas were known to be seasonally affected fishing areas where for a few months each year commercial fishing may be carried out. The trouble was and still is that these areas were known to be commercially non-viable at the time of year that the research hauls are carried out. Why was it necessary to have a special net designed and constructed for all the fleet of research ships to use? Was there no proven commercial working nets that the international fleet of research ships could have used??. Even in the areas selected that were being commercially fished why were the recorded research catches so poor?. After ten years of this annual research program with everybody using this official French designed G. O. V. trawl net, someone had the bright idea of mounting cameras on the net and they discovered that for a large percentage of the duration of each haul the ground gear of the net was not even making contact with the sea bed!!!. Comparative trials were then conducted between the Official G.O.V. net and a similar sized commercial trawl net. It was found that the G.O.V. net only caught a small percentage of the catch made by the standard commercial net. So much for the validity of the stock assessment program and the set of results that are still being used as an excuse to virtually destroy our Scottish fishing industry. Computers and computer programmes are undoubtedly vitally important to the scientist in the fish stock assessment research section. But computers are totally dependent on the information that they are fed with. In this instance I would like to suggest that they have been fed on a diet of shit and they have over the years produced an ever increasing pile of the same substance.

Looking forward in the Engine room.

Looking aft in the Engineroom.

Looking out on the working deck from the wheelhouse.

Gutting a good haul of cod while pair trawling.

Getting the Duthie trophie for best under 60 foot boat.

We did it again.

Chapter 12.

After Blondie's accident we resumed our single boat operation and enjoyed a successful period of fishing on the offshore banks east and southeast from Aberdeen. We usually landed fairly mixed catches covering a range of species with our catches always landed in very good condition. We built up a pretty good reputation and over a period of time we had a group of fish buyers buying our catches who were only looking for quality fish. Gradually more and more of our catch was purchased by this group. Working as a single boat on the banks help me to build up a detailed knowledge of a wide expanse of seabed that would prove particularly valuable once we commenced full time pair trawling. We made good catches of cod and codling on the close inshore grounds right up to the Christmas break and we finished the year as runner up for the trophy for the top earning boat in the under sixty foot class of boats in the Duthie organisation of associated fish selling companies. When we resumed fishing after the Christmas - New year break we had a very successful first trip. We went to sea a day before the rest of the inshore fleet and struck it lucky, having first chance to work on all the hard areas of ground that cod liked to gather on. We landed just short of three hundred boxes of assorted cod on only the second day's fish market of the new year and sold our catch for around ten thousand pounds. This was a good start but the weather rapidly became a problem and we made few other valuable catches during the month of January.

I was regularly in contact with an old friend and skipper on the West Coast in the Clyde, Howard McCrindle. He was a skipper who was always at the cutting edge of any new methods of working whether it be single boat mid water trawling for hake, or hunting basking sharks with a harpoon gun. Howard was always at the front of the field. He had been telling me on the phone that he was currently fishing in the mid water for hake using pelagic mid water trawl doors and a small herring mid water trawl on to which he had attached a normal white fish bag. He had described to me how he had set up his gear and was very enthusiastic about how simple it was to operate and how much money he was making. Needless to say I could take a hint and I managed to borrow a set of suitable mid water trawl doors and I had an old herring trawl in the store that was soon modified for whitefish use. We already had the net sounder gear to attach to the net that we had used in the mackerel fishery, spoken about in an earlier chapter. We did not have to put any gear ashore to try out this method of fishing. We simply chained up our normal trawl doors on deck beneath the gantry and let the pelagic door hang from our trawl gallows. Historically in late January and February each year cod gather in two very deep natural trenches in the sea bed that are found approximately ten and twenty two miles east of Aberdeen. These locations are known as the Dog Hole and the Blue Deeps. They are between eight and 10 miles long and only around half a mile wide. Very large cod historically come to these locations to spawn at this time of year. These large cod are all predators and tend to feed on smaller species of fish in the mid water. They only seem to go near the seabed for a brief period at around slack water. The Aberdeen trawler fleet always fished in the area at this time of year. If one of the boats happened to get one of these shoals of cod on the bottom right in front of their net they could make a very good catch. But it was a lottery and you could tow up and down for days on end and catch very little. I have done just that, but because we were fitted with sonar in addition to echo sounders I had been able to detect these large mature cod up off the bottom as they fed on the shoals of small fish. We set off for sea the next day and sailed off until we came to the Dog Hole. We shot our gear at the north end and proceeded to tow south. It took a bit of practice to become accustomed to operating this gear, because you had to constantly watch the net sounder and adjust the boat's speed to raise or lower the net to keep it clear of the bottom or the side walls of the deep trench, while at the same time trying to get the net to fish in the layer of water that you are observing in the sonar where the big fish are feeding. Because we were not really familiar with what we were doing we only towed our net for two hours on the first haul. We were very pleasantly surprised to find two big lifts of cod in the cod end, a very encouraging start. We managed a total of four hauls before we lost the daylight and we finally hauled up and made for the harbour to land our fish for the morning's market. Howard had told me he had found that this method of fishing was a waste of time in the dark. We managed to land two hundred and fifteen boxes of cod on the market and were well pleased with that, but one of the other boats had struck a shoal of cod on the seabed and landed more than one hundred boxes more than us from only one haul. In the morning we set off once more for the deep water but it was a poor morning with an increasing swell and a strengthening wind. I found it very difficult to control the positioning of our net and our problems were compounded by the large number of boats that were trying to operate in such a confined space. I was quite glad when darkness descended and we were able to go ashore. We had once more made a reasonable catch of some seventy boxes but I decided that we had better quit midwater fishing while we were still ahead. The chances of coming into contact with the gear of other boats while working in this confined space was just too great. The net sounder attached to the headline of the net was itself worth more than three thousand pounds and that was the first thing that was likely to be lost should we come in contact with any other gear. There was no major work required in changing back to bottom trawling. We just had to put the pelagic trawl doors ashore along with the mid water net, and reconnect our heavy trawl doors and we were ready to resume bottom fishing. While we had been involved in the mid water trawling I had observed that the larger cod visible on the sonar were frequently only some 20 feet off the seabed. This was a height that normal single boat bottom trawls would not be capable of catching them at, but in my opinion they could possibly be beneath the headline height of a large pair trawl. I discussed this with Derrick Murdoch, the skipper of the Smallwood a steel built boat of similar size and power to our own. We decided that it would be worth taking the pair bottom pair trawl gear aboard and giving it a try. A day was lost due to bad weather but that gave us the time and opportunity to get the single boat's gear ashore and the big pair trawls taken on board and everything connected up and ready for action. We went to sea next morning just before dawn and reached the north end of the Dog Hole an hour later, just as daylight was fully in. It was quite a heavy swell running but no wind and we towed south along the western edge of the deep water until we reached the south end of the hole. There we turned round and set off north. We had to alter our course from time to time to keep clear of single boats also towing in the deep water. With Smallwood and Bahati having to try and maintain a quarter-mile spread there was not a lot of space to allow boats to pass on either side when most of the length of the hole is only half a mile wide. We hauled up just before we reached the north end of the deep water to find we had a big haul of cod. Derrick on the Smallwood did not realize just how much fish there was in our net. Instead of going to the end of our cod end and starting to take some lifts of cod aboard their boat, they sailed off some distance and started to shoot their net ready to make another haul. The skipper was out on the deck and never heard me frantically calling him on the radio to tell him that we had enough fish to fill both boats. The first I heard from him was when he called us up to see why we were taking so long to come and start towing again. He found it hard to believe that our net held so much without showing just how big the catch was. By this time the wind was getting up and with the swell already present the sea state quickly worsened and we were rolling pretty badly as we were lying broadside to the motion. We had taken three lifts of fish aboard, enough to fill all our deck fish pounds, but with the heavy rolling the fish were swilling about all over the deck even higher than the gunnels of the boat and it was only our side shelter canvas sheeting that was keeping them aboard. It was getting dangerous so I shouted to the crew to open the hatch and start throwing fish down below to get some weight down below but also to give us some space on deck to take some more fish on board. Smallwood in the meantime had got their net back aboard and came up close by and took three lifts to fill their decks. They cleared their fish off their deck as quickly as possible while we were taking another three lifts aboard our boat. We were not rolling as much now with the weight of fish we had below and when Smallwood had taken enough to fill their decks again I got the crew to put the pound boards in place to close up the opening in our stern and we took the last of the fish on board us and set off for the harbour. Having to throw ungutted fish down below to enable us to get all the catch aboard caused us a hell of a lot of extra work because we had to get them back up on deck to gut and wash before stowing them on ice below in the fish hold. We set off in the direction of Aberdeen harbour with the swell on our broadside. Our deck cargo of cod was washing about alarmingly and had it not been for our canvas side screens much of the fish could have been lost over the side. We were definitely in a very unstable situation and I was truly glad once we had passed Girdleness and we began to get a bit of shelter from the swell. We made our way into the bay on the north side of Aberdeen harbour's north breakwater where we lay over the broadside and started to try and make sense out of the chaos. We brought up empty fish boxes from below deck and gutted the fish from the deck ponds into these boxes and built them up. Once we had cleared a couple of the deck ponds of fish, we started filling them up with ungutted fish being brought up from the fish room. When sufficient ungutted fish had been removed from the fish room to enable us to lay out a row of boxes, we washed the gutted fish on deck and passed them below to be boxed and iced. Gradually we made progress in gutting the catch until all the ungutted fish were back up on deck and the boat was in a more stable and controllable condition. The weather had been worsening during this time and so we decided we would make for the harbour to finish gutting and stowing the catch in more pleasant conditions. We sailed up the harbour channel and continued up into the river Dee where we berthed alongside the quay and set about finishing gutting and stowing our fish. The waste guts from the fish we were gutting were stowed in boxes on deck to be dumped over the side when we next went to sea. Having completed our work we sailed round to the fish market ready to start unloading our catch in the morning. We landed just over 400 boxes between the two boats, not a bad first haul for a new pair team. Smallwood's skipper, Derek Murdoch, and his crew were very impressed with their first haul and full of enthusiasm to continue in this new method of fishing. That was our first and last haul of big cod for that winter but we continued fishing as a team through the whole year regularly making very good catches. We fished on the offshore banks east and southeast of Aberdeen for haddock and whiting, but were constantly on the lookout for any signs of cod or codling on any areas of hard ground that we came across. Both pair trawls that we were using were fitted with ground gear that was constructed with a length of bobbins across the centre of the trawl to allow its passage over hard ground hopefully without coming fast or getting badly damaged. These bobbins are heavy solid rubber wheels with a heavy chain passing through the centre in place of an axle. The largest bobbins were 21 inches in diameter in the centre of the net and reducing to12 inches in diameter at each end of the ground gear. The bobbins were kept apart and under tension by two rubber spacers and a steel spacer with a short chain attached between each pair of bobbins to connect them to the footrope of the net. All in all it was an extremely heavy and cumbersome set of equipment, and trying to tow the gear over the hardest seabed in pursuit of cod frequently ended with the gear coming fast and the nets being quite badly damaged. However the possibility of getting a good haul of cod was normally accepted as being worth the risk. A new type of ground gear set up had recently been developed and was proving to be very effective. These were called "Rock hopper" trawls. So we decided to re-equip both boats with sets of this new type of ground gear. They were much lighter and far more flexible than the traditional bobbins and we found that we could venture over the hardest areas of seabed without suffering much damage and seldom becoming fast. As time went by and our confidence and experience in working with the pair trawls increased, we found that we were happily working in sea conditions and weather that we had never anticipated it would be possible for us to work in. But when shooting the gear and heaving up it is necessary that the two boats have to work very closely together. A heaving line has to be passed between the two boats to enable the sweeps from one side of the net to be passed to the other boat, particularly when heaving up, and your boats are subject to the heavy drag of the net. Things can get a bit dangerous as the boats cannot respond as quickly as one would like to applications of helm and throttle, but fortunately we never ever had a coming together of the boats. When there was a heavy swell running it could also be rather exciting when the other boat was alongside our net taking lifts of fish onboard. Because you only had the length of the bag and cod end in the water which resulted in the bow of the second boat coming within only a few feet away from our stern. With both boats rising up and down on the swell you had to keep the throttle handle in your hand at all times ready to nudge the boat ahead out of the danger of collision with your partner boat.. We continued working as a team right up to the Christmas break and finished the year with very good earnings. Bahati finished the year winning the trophy for the highest earning under 60 foot boat in the Arthur Duthie group of fish selling companies. We resumed our pair fishing operations when we returned to sea after the new year, but in our minds we were already wondering whether we would get any more big hauls of cod in either of the two deepwater trenches where the cod annually came to spawn in only in a few weeks time. The excitement grew in our minds as the weeks passed until both skippers were definitely suffering from "fish fever".

The Big catch story.

The story of the Bahati and Smallwood record cod catch Sunday, the 14th Feb 1982.

This story should really start on the previous Wednesday, February 10th. On that afternoon we found a good spot of fish on our echo sounder and shot our pair trawl aligned to catch that particular shoal. We towed the net for only 20 minutes before starting to haul it up. As soon as the net broke the surface it was seen to hold more fish than we have ever caught previously in a single haul. The bag full of fish only floated briefly before sinking and becoming a dead weight as is common with bags of cod.

Bahati, being rigged to lift over the stern, managed to take 200 boxes of fish on board. Even with this much weight of fish out of the net the Smallwood that lifts over the broadside, was unable to get the weight of the fish in the bag up to the surface to take any lifts of fish on board. The Smallwood then came up alongside our boat and their crew jumped across onto Bahati to assist in getting our decks cleared of fish as quickly as possible so that we could take more onboard. However the weather worsened and before the decks could be cleared of fish the net burst with the loss of all but forty boxes of the remaining fish. The loss of this fish is probably the factor that made our record catch possible.

Having landed our fish I set about modifying our net to cope with any more big bags of cod that I hoped we might catch. I extended the length of our bag with a forty five foot extension of double twine codend netting. The lestages along the entire length of the bag were securely attached onto ropes for extra strength and a set of lifting rings and a splitting becket were attached round the bag at the top end of this new netting extension. In addition we attached new four and a half inch dog ropes to the codend lifting becket and also the new splitting becket that was approximately half way along the bag. With these modifications I thought that we would be able to handle anything that we would ever be likely to catch.

Sunday the 14th was a particularly calm day. We went to sea at 9am and sailed out to the Dog Hole where a good fleet of boats were already working. We commenced to search for signs of fish working our way south but having found nothing by the time we reached the south end of the deep trench we moved seven or eight miles off to the east to the Blue Deeps, another very deep trench, to continue our search there. Then in exactly the same spot as on the previous Wednesday we found another very big shoal of cod on the seabed. We turned round and shot our net in a position so that when we ran out our wires the shoal on the seabed would be directly between our boats and therefore directly in the path of our net. In anticipation of a haul of cod at least as large as the previous Wednesday we again only continued towing for some 20 minutes. As soon as we started to haul we knew that we had a big catch because the boats didn't go ahead as we hauled as they normally do. The winch men were also having difficulties guiding the wire onto the winch drums due to the abnormally heavy strain on the trawl warps. When there was still some fifty fathoms of heavy trawl warp single sweep plus twenty fathomof spreaders still to come in before we would reach the net, the bag full of fish suddenly surfaced like a submarine. The full length of the extended section of cod end rose up out of the water like a lighthouse until we saw the splitting becket attached about half way down the bag come completed clear of the water. On top our normal codend lifter that regularly lifts about forty five boxes of fish at a time was restricted in diameter by the lifting becket and looked like a pimple stuck on the end of the bag. The vertical column of fish slowly toppled over sideways into the water while more and more of the net was coming to the surface absolutely full of fish. As quickly as possible the sweeps were hauled across from the Smallwood on our net drum pennant and a start was made to haul it in the net. The twin three-ton motors on the net drum managed to get the spreaders and the first three or four fathoms of the net on board before the weight of fish overcame them. By taking some of the weight of fish on the dog rope on the splitting becket and using the lifting tackle on the stern gantry and the net drum simultaneously we managed slowly to get the net on board until finally we saw all the foot rope and ground gear on deck. The brakes on the net drum were applied but as soon as pressure was taken off the hydraulic motors the net started to slip back. We then heaved everything back up as tight as possible again and using long steel poles through the brake wheels as levers for tightening the brakes on the net drum, we screwed up the brakes even harder. To no avail. As soon as we took the pressure off the hydraulic motors the gear would begin to slide back. Finally to secure the bag I used a mooring rope made fast to the base of the after gantry. I passed the rope round and round the bag and then round the gantry until I had five folds in place securing the bag to the gantry base. As soon as we released the hydraulic motors the net slipped back but to my relief my compound lashing held.

We could now turn our attention to trying to get some fish on board. We heaved in on the splitting becket dog rope and till we brought the cod end section of the bag to the surface. This whole sixty-five foot section of bag was packed solid to bursting point. The Smallwood then manoeuvred alongside this section of bag with the intention of trying to take a lift of fish on board to allow some working space in the net. This idea proved futile however because the Smallwood lifts over the broadside and with the weight of fish in the bag being so great that any attempt to lift merely listed the boat's rails down to the water level, the cod ends remaining apparently unmoved. We therefore heaved upon the cod end rope hauling the lifting strap to the stern of Bahati and hooked on our lifting tackle. We then let go the strain on the dog rope to the splitting becket in the hope that this would allow some of the fish to run further back down the bag so that we could get some fish aboard. Another failure, as soon as all the strain was past to our lifting tackle the hook on the expensive tufnol block just straightened and fell out. A new set of steel eight inch lifting tackle blocks was then attached to our stern lifting gantry complete with a brand new braided nylon tackle rope. With this new tackle in place we did manage to get three lifts of fish on board. While attempting to make the fourth lift however the new nylon lifting tackle rope broke. The resultant sudden load coming on the two dog ropes was too much for them and they both in turn broke with reports like two gunshots in quick succession.

The total weight of the catch was now hanging from our gantry leg. When I went aft to assess the situation I began to appreciate just how much weight there was in the net. When I looked over the stern I could see that there were only two and a half planks of freeboard left above water at our stern. Bahati had an eighteen foot wide transom stern and was being hauled that far down into the water by the weight of the catch. Had the boat been built with the more traditional pointed stern I think that there was a very good chance it would have foundered. Now the only remaining chance of landing our catch was to try and tow our net and catch to Stonehaven harbour in the hope that we might manage with the help of the high tide to get it grounded onto the beach there. A start was made to attempt this tow. The engine revs were gradually increased until we had reached our normal towing speed. We were going ahead but steering was impossible as the weight and drag of the catch was well off-centre, even with full counter helm we still turned slowly to port. A rope was passed to the Smallwood and with the Smallwood leading the way we set off in the direction of Stonehaven. The tow started at three thirty in the afternoon and we reached Stonehaven Bay at twelve thirty that night. As we approached Stonehaven harbour and the water began to shallow we thought there might be a danger of the net snagging on the sea bed so we stopped the boats. During the evening while we had been towing the catch towards land I telephoned home and spoke to my eldest son telling him that there was a brand-new net in our store. I instructed him to go down to the store and cut the bag off this net at a specific point that I described to him. I also told him to splice a brand-new dog rope onto the cod end lifter. He was then to take the bag and rope down to my brother's headquarters at the harbour. My younger brother Hamish was the boss of the marine survival training centre based at Stonehaven harbour. Once we were stationary in the bay my brother Hamish came out to us in one of the rescue craft bringing my new bag and cod end with him. We attached the new bag and cod end to the bag that had the fish in, by joining the two bags together at a point immediately above where the lashing was. My brother had arrived complete with wetsuit and gas bottles and proceeded to drive down to the net and join up our two broken dog ropes underwater in the dark. When all was ready we streamed the new cod end and bag out in the tide and took some strain on the now repaired splitting becket dog rope. With everyone standing well clear we then cut our five strands of mooring rope at the foot of the gantry that had brought out net and catch this far. Relieved of the weight the stern of our boat suddenly bobbed up. We steadily heaved up on the dog rope to the splitting becket. Once this becket was heaved up to deck level at the stern of our boat it was made fast. We then set about hauling in the net above this becket as there was now some free netting available to recover. When we had hauled in as much of the new second bag as we could we again secured it to the stern of the boat. We now had two bags of fish secured to our stern like a pair of trousers. This had halved the strain on each bag but just as importantly it had halved the length of the bags trailing in the water and liable to damage by the seabed. At high tide just after seven in the morning we finally made it into the harbour. The fish were so tightly packed in the nets that we still found it impossible to get any aboard the boats. A very large mobile crane was then hired from Aberdeen and set up at the end of one pier. It managed to haul the catch part way across the harbour, and finally at high tide in the evening it succeeded in dragging both bags of cod onto the beach close to the slipway. There the receding tide left two mountainous bags of cod high and dry on the beach. The two boats' crews along with many of local helpers managed to handle and box nearly 1000 hundredweight boxes of cod ready for Aberdeen fish market next morning. The remainder of the catch was cleared from the beach as the tide went out on next morning. At the final tally it was shown that we had landed at total 1632 boxes of cod all caught on one 20 minute tow. A truly never to be forgotten experience.

Bahati and partner boat Darona in Aberdeen.

Another deck full of cod.

Smallwood tries to get bag of cod to split.

The last of the record catch
waiting for the tide to ebb on
the second morning to allow
the last of the catch to be landed
from the second half of the
two bags that we towed ashore.

Chapter 13.

Smallwood and Bahati caught another three hundred and forty boxes of cod in the same week after the record haul but I was not there to see it and the crew managed very well on their own. My mother-in-law had died in Shetland on the day we made our big catch. I had only managed to get the boats and the bags of cod into the harbour before I had to set off for the airport to fly to Shetland with Lilian. The following morning I went down to an associated fish salesman's office in Lerwick to see just how much fish we had managed to get onto the Aberdeen fish market that morning. They phoned our office in Aberdeen and were told that just under one thousand boxes had reached the market. I said I was a bit disappointed with that, but the salesman laughed and said that they were estimating that they had processed just more than half of the total catch. We attended Lilian's mother's funeral and completed all the other formalities that have to be undertaken at a time like this. We returned to Aberdeen on the early morning flight on the Friday and I was able to get to the fish salesman's office in time to complete the settling up. That was the last of the really huge hauls of fish in the deep water for that year, and they were never to be seen again right up to the present day. We continued as a pair team however and continued to make good landings almost every week. We had one notable exception however. After the big catch I think that we believed that we had catching cod mastered. We knew that we were faced with the hungry month of March at home, so when I heard from Howard McCrindle that the cod were just coming on in the Firth of Clyde I had a chat with Derek, the skipper of the

Smallwood, and we decided we would make a move to the west coast through the Caledonian canal and see if we could have some success catching Clyde cod. Our voyage to the west was uneventful. I think this in its self must be a first for me. Once we sailed through Sanda Sound and into the Clyde we started to look for signs of fish, I regret to say without any success. We then decided just to shoot our gear and try a tow and see if we would stumble across any marks of fish as we towed. We did not tow for very long before we came fast and had to heave back to get our gear hauled. We had not come fast on an object. We had just dug our ground gear and net into the seabed mud. We sailed on to another area of shallower water in the hope that things would be better there but once more we came fast to the bottom. Having fished in the Clyde with the little Bahati for several years in the past I thought that I had a fair amount of knowledge of the fishing grounds there. But at that time I had been seine netting or prawn trawling with a single boat and you could avoid or tow round undulations on the seabed with these types of gear. Now with our pair trawl gear and our boats keeping a quarter of a mile apart while working with a minimum of one hundred fathoms of wire on the sea floor. This, plus the big net and heavy ground gear meant that any little hill on the sea bed between the boats was enough to stop us. On our normal harder grounds on the east coast we simply increased power and we would, nine times out of ten, get the gear to spring free and we continued on your way. Here in the Clyde if you started to slow down and you increased power you invariably just pulled the ground gear and net deeper into the mud. We certainly were not catching any worthwhile quantities of fish and with worsening weather we went into the harbour at Troon to moor up our boats there and go home for the weekend. We hired a minibus for the weekend so that both boats crews could be accommodated in the one vehicle along with our boats' orders of food and other things we would require to transport back to Troon for going to sea on the following week. I had a lengthy telephone conversation with Howard McCrindle when home at the weekend and he gave me some suggestions as to where we might find some harder grounds which would be more suitable for our method of fishing. When we went to sea on the Monday we set off south along the coast to an area they call the Balantrae Banks off Garvin. Howard had suggested that the seabed there was much harder and more in keeping with what we were used to working over on the East Coast. At certain times of year these grounds are known to be very prolific and are major spawning ground for herring. Traditionally big landings of herring had been made in this area with ring nets and herring trawlers. Now was not the time however, and at this time of year the cod are mainly looking for deeper water in which to spawn. From the experience the previous week we knew that trying to fish these waters with the very muddy bottom was not going to be a possibility for us, and so we tried a few hauls over these shallower and harder grounds. We did catch thirty boxes of fish on one haul but there was not the quantity or the quality of fish that we required to keep our pair of boats operating viably and so we decided that we had done enough and set sail to return to the East Coast. Our short trip to the West Coast had been a dead loss financially but it certainly proved to us just what sort of sea beds were not suitable for pair trawling over with our weight of gear. As soon as we were back at Aberdeen and playing on our own pitch we were able to maintain our consistent level of landings. By late spring we were concentrating our efforts on the offshore banks once more. Usually we sailed off to The Edge or the outside of the Turbot Bank on Sunday night and gradually worked our way ashore. We normally made a landing on a Wednesday morning and again on Friday. Our catches were principally made up of haddock and whiting but we never neglected towing over any areas of really hard bottom in the hope of gathering up some cod. We were successful on more than a few occasions with hauls of over 200 boxes of big cod being made on the Turbot Bank and at the north end of the Aberdeen Bank. We also had two very successful trips to the 74-mile bank. On the first occasion we filled both boats to capacity with cod and codling all caught on our first and only tow. On that occasion we saw the marks of fish on the bottom and didn't tow for very long. It was a beautiful very hot summer day and so we only took the fish aboard a couple of lifts at a time so that they were not too long on deck in the heat before they were gutted and stowed below on ice. It took about six hours to get every thing on board and iced in the fish rooms, but by keeping the catch alongside swimming in the net until we could handle the fish in small quantities, the quality of our catch was kept very good. By October we were concentrating our efforts on the inshore grounds south of Aberdeen and again, weather permitting, we were able to make a very steady living. Our ever-growing experience in working as a pair team and keeping our ground gear well adjusted for maximum efficiency allowed us to work regularly over grounds that a single boat trawler had great difficulties working on. Similarly we could find ourselves continuing to work in sea states that we would not earlier have thought possible. On one occasion while fishing south of Stonehaven the swell had been growing all day but we had no wind and every four hours when we heaved up we had been taking on board three or four lifts of fish. We had shot away to start a tow just after dark and while there was a heavy swell it was not in the least uncomfortable. It was only when we started heaving up that we realize just how high the swell had grown. As we began to close to within heaving line distance I was amazed to find that I was completely losing sight of the fully lit Smallwood apart from its mast headlight every time a swell passed between us. Any direct contact between the two boats with this level of swell could have been calamitous for both boats particularly with one built of wood and the other steel. We had another quite good haul and there was a temptation to shoot again, but discretion got the better of valour and so once the fish had been taken aboard the two boats we set sail for Aberdeen. Once we were underway and sailing at cruising speed we could appreciate just how big a swell was running. As we neared Aberdeen we could hear the harbour control speaking to vessels about to leave or enter the harbour and informing them of the poor conditions at the harbour bar where the strong flow of the river Dee enters the sea at the mouth of the harbour. We got permission to enter the harbour but were warned to be very cautious as the sea conditions over the bar were considered to be dangerous. We approached the pier heads slowly with each swell picking us up and rolling us forward. It's quite difficult to steer a boat at these reduced speeds and I was having to devote all my attention to trying to maintain a steady course up the channel while

George, my mate on the Bahati, was standing behind me looking aft out over the stern and telling me when the next wave was going to pick us up and drive us forward. With half the stern of the boat being open to deck level there was always a chance that an unusually steep wave could come sweeping on board, but this happened only once and the water quickly cleared off the deck. We continued working on these hard inshore grounds up to the Christmas break when we stopped for 10 days holiday before returning to sea a few days after the new year. For the second year in succession Bahati was to win the Duthie Organisation's cup for the top earning under sixty foot boat in their fleet. I could not believe that our success would continue as we were constantly being told of the dire state of our fish stocks and the need for the enforcement of ever smaller catch quotas. I have mentioned earlier just how much it cost to work out of Aberdeen because of the charges for dock labour which you had no way of avoiding. In this particular year we had to pay a total of fifty six thousand pounds for dock labour between the two boats. When you think that we were quite prepared to do this work ourselves, as was normal in all the other harbours, you will appreciate just how much the crews resented seeing these charges being deducted from our earnings each week.

Chapter 14.

When we returned to sea after the New Year we made two quite good landings as the cod had gathered together over the patches of extremely hard ground during the Christmas break. The cod had not been disturbed by fishing boats over this period. We were of course by now thinking about the big cod in the deep water trenches once more, but we must have caught them all the previous year because they never materialized, and never have returned to their historic haunts right up to the present day. We continued working as a pair through the early spring and up to the beginning of May never making any spectacular catches but at least managing to make a living wage for the crew each week, unless we were kept ashore by bad weather. Then Smallwood had to undergo a board of trade survey and stability trials and it was found that she failed to meet the new standards laid down for steel vessels of her class. This meant that she had to cease fishing immediately and would not be allowed to resume fishing until she had undergone considerable modification in a shipyard. In these circumstances we had no option other than to find a new pair trawl partner.

This was not a very difficult task with the high and consistent level of landings we had made with Smallwood there was no shortage of willing volunteer partners. I decided to team up with another Aberdeen boat of our own size and horsepower called the Darona. She was skippered and owned by Abbey Walker who had a proven single boat catch performance record and so we saw no reason why we could not make another successful team. From the first time we went to sea we experience no unexpected problems working as a team. With both boats having the same Volvo engines and both winches being hydraulic with infinite variable hauling speeds it was much easier than working in unison with Smallwood. We worked all the usual offshore grounds and caught a lot of fish but things were now getting much more difficult on the quota front. You had to be constantly calling ashore to check up on what the current situation was and how much you were still allowed to land for that week. When we had caught our week's quota for one species we would try to move grounds in the hope of avoiding catching more of that species.

This was no certainty and frequently we either had to dump the unwanted fish dead or if there was a single boat in the area and they had not caught their quota of that species we preferred simply to let them come and take the unwanted fish from our net.

Life was bad enough at sea but more and more I was to find myself attending meetings with departmental fisheries officials and politicians. Several times I had to travel to London and Westminster as a member of an official delegation tasked with lobbying MPs on fisheries matters. Nothing could be a more frustrating and thankless task. It is impossible to meet MPs from more than one political party at any time if you want to get any headway made at all. You may want to discuss issues of vital relevance to the fishing industry but if members of more than one party are present any sensible consideration of the industry's problems goes right out of the window. All the MPs are only interested in trying to score political points against each other and the situation that you are trying to have a meaningful exchange of views on gets completely forgotten. Having to conduct at least three and frequently four repeat meetings with different parties is bad enough, but when you know within yourself that the people you are meeting with could not care less about any problem. While they may side with you at the time of your meeting they think absolutely nothing of voting in an entirely opposite direction at the first opportunity. I used to get very depressed seeing first hand just how poor the calibre of many of our elected MPs really was. The number of members who only seemed to inhabit the bars in Westminster I found quite amazing. The only time they seemed to take any part in proceedings was when the division bells rang and they would go shuffling off mumbling about their disturbance and were guided by their whips to pass through which ever lobby their party required. I often used to say that if these people could actually get people to vote for them then we can only blame our selve for the state of our government and we must obviously get the government we deserve. I remember on one occasion coming home singularly depressed and describing our day in Westminster with many of its members as being the closest thing to the annual open day at the local mental hospital. The know-all attitude of many of the inhabitants of this institution was quite breathtaking, only being surpassed by their lack of understanding of the real world and the effect that their administration can bring to bear on the working population. The old adage of the American Indians "that white man speaks with forked tongue" can frequently and justifiably be applied to many members of this hallowed house. They all promise the earth when in opposition but as soon as they come to power they become reliable lobby fodder voting faithfully on party instruction regardless of any prior commitments or undertakings. I have found over time that I could create a far greater discomfort to the government institutions by using the public media and releasing factual details and exposure on any confrontational situation that the government of whatever persuasion were trying to keep covered up with ever more political spin.

We fished on quite successfully up to late autumn always managing to catch our full quota of haddock and whiting each month, and often catching all our allocation of cod as well. The prices were not that good while our costs seemed to be constantly on the increase. Fuel in particular by that time was costing each boat around one thousand pounds a week and because we were regularly landing relatively large numbers of boxes of fish on each landing the labour cost to pay for dock labour was getting beyond the joke as well. We decided to try to concentrate on cod and codling because these fish brought better prices. These species however are normally found on the hardest of sea bed areas and so you have to balance the improved value of your catch against the greatly increased costs of working on these net and gear destroying grounds. You could very easily find yourself in effect buying your catch due to the increased costs of working these grounds compared to the costs of working on easier grounds for a less valuable catch. We normally worked south and south east of Aberdeen but we did go north a couple of times to very hard patches of ground off Fraserburgh and west towards Macduff. These patches of ground we were told were very bad and the single boats that normally worked this area reported coming fast a lot and doing lots of damage to their gear. We must have experienced beginners' luck because in three days we caught just over seven hundred boxes of codling. We actually ran out of empty boxes and ice and had to go into Fraserburgh for more boxes and ice to enable us to stow all our catch before setting off for the market in Aberdeen. The following week we returned to this ground but did not get much fish at all and shattered one net. We went east with our tail between our legs and shot on the inside edge of the "Hole of the Broch" and towed east on that edge of the deep water. With the sonar you are able to follow the edges of the contours of the deep water very easily but we were not seeing many signs of fish. We were therefore very happy to find a catch of seven lifts of cod when we hauled up. That was enough to make the difference between success and failure for that week. With disruptive weather it got progressively harder to make a good living each week but we stuck it out till the Christmas break.

Chapter 15.

The Darona in the mean time was due for a major refit and so we returned to single boat trawling for some months. On a couple of occasions we teamed up with other boats for several weeks when their regular partner boats were broken down or having refits. This was fine up to a point, but more and more of the fleet were being sold because escalating costs and ever smaller quotas were making it harder and harder to remain profitable. The skipper of the Darona decided he had had enough because he was offered a good job ashore and thought that he would be better to sell up as well. Without a regular dependable partner I started to think along the lines of giving up as well. I loved fishing when I was pitting my wits against nature in the form of fish stocks and weather but life was becoming more a battle with regulations and officialdom and ever spiralling costs. As a director of the Fisherman's Federation I was a party to all the talks about fish stock assessments and likely quotas that were going to be imposed along with the introduction of limited days at sea. We had always battled against limited days at sea due to bad weather but having to stay ashore in good weather to satisfy some beurocrat was the last straw. We were going to be forced to work in dangerous conditions hazarding our boat and crew because we could not go ashore once we had gone to sea without losing the fishing time allocated to us. I made the final decision to sell up in mid February. I had built my boat to fish within 30 miles of the shore in winter time while happy to range over a hundred miles off in summer. Now in mid February I was to find myself fishing in the Devil's Hole a hundred and ten miles out in the middle of the North Sea simply because of commercial pressure and the pressure of knowing that five families were depending on me catching enough fish to pay the wages to support them. The 2 o'clock forecast told us that we were to have north-westerly severe to storm force gales imminent so I called out the crew and we heaved up and got all our gear on board and lashed everything down securely and set of for home as darkness came down. In the worsening weather I was on watch all through the night my self as we shuddered and banged our way towards the shore. We were reduced to a crawl as we battled through the heavy seas taking close on 17 hours to reach port safely. That gave me plenty of time to think of my situation and come to the conclusion that I should look into the possibility of selling up and finding something else to do with my life. As soon as we reached the shore I left the crew with the boat and went up into the city to see my accountants. I wanted to know how I would be financially if I sold the boat. There I was given the comforting news that I would have to give the tax man about two thirds of any price I could get for my boat unless I could roll over my cash into any new venture I might set up. The only other way there was of keeping more of my hard earned money was to keep working the boat till I was sixty years old when I would then get an allowance on any sale. I had heard enough and went down to our salesman's office and said I wanted to get out now and to see about selling up. I only owned one third of the boat but the other share holders were happy to follow my wishes. And so the boat was sold and I could go ashore and think about what I was going to do.

I still had my salmon fishing company with my partner Ian More that my sons had been operating in their school and university holidays and I was considering whether it would be possible to expand this operation and make it a stand alone business. With this in view I went to see the man at the top of the salmon research program to hear from him if there was any concerns as to the state of our salmon stocks and if it was likely that moves could be made to try to curtail this historic fishery. He assured me that all the rivers in Scotland were producing the maximum number of young fish to go to sea each year that they were capable of supporting. Therefore there should be no reason for reducing the annual catch of mature fish as allowing more fish to go up the rivers to spawn only resulted in higher mortality of the young fish because the biology of the rivers could not provide more life support than it was already doing. With this advice and endorsement ringing in my ears I made the decision to try and expand my salmon fishing business. I was told by my accountants that I would be able to roll over my money from the sale of my boat into this business and therefore could postpone having to give any more tax than necessary to the government at that time.

We had managed to secure the lease of a section of the coast in Burghead Bay the previous year and my sons had managed to make a reasonable catch there in their holidays. It was conveniently close to the Hopeman fishery that we were already working and I thought that if I operated the combined fishery for the full season I was certain to have a viable business. I therefore went about buying all the equipment such as a salmon cobble with nets and anchors along with a tractor and other necessary equipment to run this new venture. We managed to acquire all the equipment in time to be ready for the opening of the new salmon fishing season. To buy all this equipment I had to use most of the money from my share of the sale of Bahati. This did not bother me because I knew I had to spend it on vital business related materials to qualify for rollover of my capital into my new business.

Although I had been working on the salmon fishing for more than 15 years all my experience was on what we call a "rock station." That is a fishery that is conducted in deep water from a boat. Our new location in Burghead bay was a beach station which was tidal and when we started it had previously been worked from the shore using a tractor rather than a boat. Once again a steep learning curve lay ahead of us. The sandy beach was very flat and from low water mark to the top of the tidemark on the shore was over three hundred yards.

I think at this point I should try to describe a traditional salmon net and how it operates. Basically salmon tend to swim along our coasts and so to catch them you can only use legally approved methods. You traditionally have to stretch a barrier of net running from high water mark seawards this is to divert the fish seawards to try to find a way round the net to continue its journey. This section of the net is called " The Leader." At its seaward end it is attached to the entrance to what is called "The Bag." This is basically a triangular shaped net or trap where the fish pass through two reducing openings until they find themselves in what is called the fish court. Here they can swim round and round without escaping until you take the catch out of the net. The operation of these nets is controlled by many laws which govern construction, mesh sizes , a weekly closed time when no fishing can take place, along with annual seasons when no fishing is allowed. When operating at a rock station the leader stretches from a shore attachment point to the mouth of the bag net. It is supported by floats along its length and swings about clear of the bottom. On a beach station however it is an entirely different business. You have to set up a line of poles across the sand until you reach the position of the bagnet. These poles have to be pumped into the sand to a depth of at least 6 feet under the surface of the beach and have to have guy ropes to each side to keep them vertical and in position. The leader of the net has then to be stretched along the sand until it reaches the bag net and must be attached to the top and bottom of these poles to keep it in position. This means that virtually all work carried out while operating a sand station is governed to a major extent to the varying times of the tidal range. The law governing the weekly closed time, when we started in this new fishery, meant that we could not set up the nets until after 6 am on a Monday morning and all nets had to be closed up so as not to be capable of catching fish by 12 mid day on Saturday. This meant that because of the tidal conditions every second week we could not get the shoremost net operating until Monday afternoon while we would have to render it incapable of catching any fish by late Friday night. This detail about legal fishing times comes to the fore in future chapters.

Chapter 16.

We started getting the beach prepared for fishing as soon as the legal season started on February 11th. Setting up all the poles on the beach to carry our leaders was backbreaking work as well as being bloody freezing. You use a small portable water pump which is attached to a lance like pipe with a nozzle on the end. You have to stand the twenty foot high pole on end in the desired position and then hold the water lance alongside the pole. The jet of water from the pump liquifies the sand under the pole and you simply let the pole along with the lance find its own way down into the sand until the required depth is reached, then you remove the lance and turn off the pump. Very simple to explain but not so easy in practice with obstructions feet down in the sands. It was so cold that the pump was filling up with ice slush and had to be stopped to be cleaned out and restarted. Despite our best water proof clothing with water flying up as well as down you became almost hypothermic in a remarkably short time. By the end of the first week we had the beach set up ready to start fishing with 2 nets at the beginning of the second week. After two days and only a handful of salmon caught the frost jumped and just as suddenly we had a gale of north west wind directly on to the beach. The result was everything we had done was torn up out of the sand and was washed up the beach and finished up at high tide mark looking like gigantic bundles of knitting with twenty foot needles entangled in the midst.

This disaster dampened our enthusiasm more than a little and we decided not to set up the nets again until the weather promised to be a bit more settled. We did not waste our time however as we set about constructing some more nets and leaders which we would require anyway later in the season. We heard from another salmon fisherman about a new type of bag net that he had developed called a double headed bag. This was to our knowledge the first serious modification that had been made to traditional salmon nets for many decades . He swore that they had multiplied his catches and we knew from the local grapevine just how much salmon he had been landing. We therefore set about making a couple of these nets so that we could try them out. They proved to be just as efficient as we had been told but were of course twice as much bulk as our single nets and our 21 foot cobble could only hold one net at a time. This was going to make getting all the nets to sea and set up and fishing on a Monday morning far too time consuming. We heard about a bigger salmon cobble that was for sale on the east coast at Eyemouth and travelled all the way down there to see it only to find a heap of rubbish and had to return home empty handed. The two double nets we had made were catching more fish than the other eight traditional nets were when added together, but with our small cobble they were a hell of a struggle to operate. I then heard of a 26 foot cobble for sale at Cullen only about thirty miles away. We went down and had a look at it and managed to buy it. It was old but in not bad condition and I had been able to speak to the big salmon company that had built it and operated it for many years and they said that it should see us in good stead for quite a few more years to come. I duly sailed the boat back to Burghead with a couple of the lads and found that it made life far easier. We could take all ten leaders out on one trip on a Monday morning and take them all ashore in one load at the close of fishing for any week. We were kept going flat out operating the gear we had and just did not have time to make any more of the double bags for that season but were convinced that all our nets would be of this type before the next fishing season. We finished the season having caught far more fish than we had ever done before but the prices had not been very good due to the market being saturated with farmed fish. We had done well but decided to use the money to have ten of the new double bags made for us to our specification by Sellars, the salmon fishing company, of Macduff, along with new 50 fathom leaders for every net. With this expensive amount of equipment we were confident that the next season would really be a record breaker for us. Our landlords knew of our catches and demanded an increase in rent for the coming season up to £9000 but this did not bother us too much as we were confident that our new gear would absorb this additional overhead without problem. They were they said discussing offering us a ten year lease at this annual figure and we told them that this would be acceptable to us. We had learned our lesson well from the previous season and decided not to start fishing until later in the spring when we hoped the weather might be more dependable.

In salmon fishing all your gear is at the mercy of the elements and is uninsurable. Once you are set up and fishing you have a minimum of twenty thousand pounds worth in the sea and at risk at any one time. On a beach station your gear and equipment is also vulnerable to vandals and thieves. Somebody with a sharp knife and evil intent can cause you thousands of pounds in damage in a matter of minutes. The shore nets are also vulnerable to persons stealing you catch if you are not on constant watch during the vulnerable hours of each tide.

On one occasion on our first season while my sons were working Burghead Bay, my eldest son was driving along the beach in our little Ferguson tractor at 3.30 in the morning to fish our shore net when he saw two men taking fish from our net. It was a dull hazy morning and they did not hear him approaching because of the noise of the waves on the beach. He was nearly up to them before they realised and they immediately ran off up the beach towards the forest that runs right along the top of this beach. Now my son having seen what they were doing was hopping mad. He may only have been 17 years old but at six feet four and big with it and with wild hair down to his shoulders he jumped off the tractor and set of in pursuit. Despite being hampered by wearing chest waders and size 13 overboots he was quickly catching them up. Seeing what was happening they split up so that he could only chase one of them. This he did for some time until the man finally collapsed on the ground unable to continue any further. My son must have been a rather frightening site in his furious rage as he stood over the exhausted man because the man suddenly shit himself and was full of apologies for what he had done. My son told him to get up and go down to the beach where he got him to sit on the platform on the back of the tractor while he then drove to the phone box at Burghead harbour and called the police. When the police arrived and saw the state of the man they were at first concerned as to what my son must have done to the guy to get him into a state like he was in. But that was soon sorted out and they took the guy away. When it came to court his excuse was that they had been bird watching, but that did not wash with the court in the same way as his trousers had washed.

We started fishing at the beginning of April and only put in a limited amount of gear to start with so as not to hazard too much of our resources until the catches of salmon warranted it. We still had not got the promised ten year lease signed up but did not think too much of it. At this time we heard about a salmon fishery for sale at Portmahomack, in the entrance to the Dornoch firth. It had been owned and operated by the same family for close on a hundred years but the present owners and operators were beyond retirement age and had decided to sell as they had no family to carry it on. My partner and I discussed the situation and decided that if we could buy this fishing we would always have something to call our own that we could fall back on if anything went wrong with continuing the leases at Hopeman and Burghead. We went across to Portmahomack a couple of times to look at the location in various conditions and when satisfied with our impressions we arranged to meet up with the owners to see formally over the property and possibly put in an offer. We came to a tentative agreement and got copies of the deeds of ownership and exact definitions of boundaries and demarcation points. The deeds to the property were old Scottish crown deeds predating the union of Scotland and England and we were advised that they were totally secure and legal. They extended sea wards to a point in the middle of the Dornoch firth and granted the holder of the title the sole right to fish legally for salmon in all this area. We had to go to our bank to see if they would finance the purchase and this they agreed to if we lodged the title of the property with them for security. We then reached an agreement on price and we bought the fishings along with the equipment on the fishery. We would take over the fishery for the next season which would give us time to get everything we needed into place.

To work this fishery we needed somewhere to live in Portmahomack during the fishing season and so we searched for and bought a cottage with a piece of land adjoining to build a store on to hold our gear. We also had to buy another large cobble to enable us to work the type of gear that we were going to use on this fishery. We were glad we had an understanding bank supporting us but were confident in our future with our expanding company.

We had our best season ever with the Hopeman and Burghead Bay fisheries that year, so good in fact that we like idiots paid off the bank in full by the end of the season and still made some money.

Chapter 17.

It was at this point that things started to go pear shaped. The tax men decided that all the equipment I had bought for the expanded fishery with my roll over capital would not be accepted as assets as it was too vulnerable to be considered for rollover allowances. This meant I had a big tax bill to pay. To add insult to injury the b----rds then classified the equipment purchased as capital gains which we could only claim a depreciation rate on for any tax relief. In addition the purchase of the other fishery and assets were deemed to be capital gains because we had paid off the bank debt. The tax man can really screw you when he sets his mind on it. We could only hope that the coming season could be equally good if we were to get over this set back.

It was around this time that some chinless wonder in the House of Lords started a move to review the laws related to salmon fishing. The value of river fishings and rents were soaring and the rich landowners on their estates started to think if they could only get rid of coastal netsmen the increased numbers of fish that they believed would be found in their rivers would make them a fortune. There was no other reason for trying to get rid of legal netsmen other than greed. Land owners and netsmen owned their titles with equal legal rights. Why should one group be penalised while the other was to profit. With Mrs Thatcher and her political backers from the upper house they had an easy ride. They decided that they would simply extend the weekly closed time for netting and by that means render commercial fishing inviable. In addition to extending the weekly closed time they were to introduce a law that only allowed you to fish within 300 yds of low water mark. This would mean that on our Portmahomack fishery we would lose the use of 85% of the area legally owned by our title. There was to be no compensation for losses resulting from this legislation.

Earlier in the book you will have learned that I had been a director of the Scottish Fisheries Federation working to try to support our sea fishermen. When I left the White Fish Federation and gave up my directorship there, it was only a brief time before I was to find myself on the executive council of the Scottish Salmon Net Fishermen's Association. This long established organisation had been set up to support Scottish legal salmon netsmen. I was soon to find myself at the forefront of the meetings and negotiations that were taking place between all the interested parties. We had the economics of the commercial salmon fishing business studied in detail by accountants and their conclusion was that should the extension of weekly closed time come to pass most salmon fishing would become commercially non-viable with almost immediate effect.

We also had the top salmon biologists look into the supposed problem of declining salmon stocks to find out if there was any justification for reducing the annual salmon catch. These top scientists came back and reported that with the exception of a few rivers in south-west Scotland all the other rivers in Scotland were producing the maximum number of immature fish ready to go to sea that they were capable of producing. The biology of each river is the total life-support system for the immature fish growing in the river. Any river can only provide life-support for a given number of immature fish. This is proven by the fact that the number of immature fish going to sea annually from any river remains almost a constant while the number of mature fish that are ascending the river to spawn can vary considerably year by year. Allowing more mature fish to go up the river to spawn simply means that there will be a higher mortality rate amongst the immature fish. Because of this competitive environment the immature fish surviving to go to sea will be less well developed and of a smaller size making their survival when they first enter salt water much more hazardous.

Allowing to many mature fish to go up the river to spawn can also cause its own its problems. There is only a fixed area of suitable spawning beds in any river. If too many fish reach the spawning grounds, in the resulting competition for space many of the eggs that have already been laid are killed off by being exposed by other fish trying to spawn on top of the existing reds in the same area. Traditionally river boards speak about salmon rivers filling with fish from the top. This is because the high-value large spring salmon enter the river first and make their way upstream to the highest spawning grounds. The smaller summer salmon and grilse spread throughout the length of the river. The salmon scientists know from their studies that like begets like when salmon breed. The most valuable large spring salmon which used to be exclusive to the upper spawning grounds ensured that their progeny maintained that valuable proportion of the river's total stock. When the river system is overstocked with fish many of the male grilse fight their way much higher up the rivers to the spawning beds that used to be exclusive to the valuable mature spring salmon. These smaller fish have been in fresh water for a much shorter time and are much more active and in better condition and they interbreed actively with much bigger hen fish. The resulting progeny will always however develop to become summer salmon or grilse which in turn reduces the numbers of spring salmon in the river.

I had previously worked with Peter Carr, an internationally known television film maker, when he made a Fragile Earth Series film about the effects of the increasing grey seal population and the effects it was having on our fish stocks and fishing industry. I had appeared in the film but had also spent a great deal of time helping with providing evidence and scientific contacts to assist in making his film. I now contacted him and explained the situation we found ourselves in regarding the proposed punitive legislation. He at once set about getting finance and a contract to make another Fragile Earth feature to expose the one sided and scientifically unsupported legislation that was afoot supposedly to help the survival of our native Atlantic salmon stocks. He duly made his documentary and it was shown on the BBC. It got plenty of media coverage at the time but I regret to say that it only helped to delay the move to bring in the proposed new legislation.

By this time I found myself having been elected onto two river fishery boards, the Findhorn river board and the much more important Kyle of Sutherland river board which was responsible for looking after the five major salmon rivers flowing into the Dornoch Firth. I was elected on to both river boards to be the representative of the commercial salmon fishing proprietors under the boards' control. In addition to my position on these boards I had been appointed to the Highland Water Purification Board for five years as the Secretary of State's nominee representing all sectors of the fishing industry, both white fish and salmon. My membership of these public bodies was like in effect having a foot in both camps. I could easily gauge how the opinions of the various landowners were shaping up. It soon became very obvious that the estates belonging to the old wealth and traditional lairds did not want change. They looked on the ownership of their estates as only having custody over them for their lifetime. But they were responsible for looking after and passing on their estates to future generations in as good a state as possible. These lairds were almost all fully in support of there being no need to change the law as commercial netting interests had for centuries worked constructively with the landowners to the maintenance of the quality of the rivers and the salmon stocks in them. It had never been in the nets men's interest to over fish any river or salmon stock in it. Alternatively the new-money estate owners almost without exception could not get rid of the netsmen quickly enough. Their eyes and brains were rolling like cash machines calculating up how much more their investments would be worth once the netsmen were gone.

Chapter 18.

With these concerns ever present we continued fishing on our three fishing stations but in each of them we were experiencing ever increasing problems with marauding grey seals. The seal numbers in the inner Moray Firth were increasing at a dramatic rate. The large Moray Firth salmon fishing company which had controlled the vast majority of the coast for generations had ceased to operate. This company throughout its years of operation normally shot over 1000 seals a year on their various fisheries. Now after four years without this cull taking place the seal numbers were getting completely out of hand. At Portmahomack, for example, traditionally there were four netting points on the length of the 2 1/2 miles of coast that we owned. We were forced by seal predation to reduce this to only one line of nets. Even then I had to erect a 24 feet high scaffolding tower at low water mark with a small hut on top so that a marksman could sit there and try to protect our nets during daylight hours. With this reduced effort and increased costs we were only just managing to clear our costs and we were certainly were not making anything on our investment. At Hopeman it was a very similar story. We had operated three lines of nets along the mile and a half of coast that we controlled but we were forced to reduce this first from 3 to 2 and finally to only one line of nets. We tried the mechanical and sonic seal scaring devices that were available at the time, but I regret to say in our particular conditions in relatively shallow water these proved to be a complete waste of time despite their high cost. The Burghead fishery was still doing quite well but it was having to keep the other two fisheries afloat.

Our friendly contacts within government had been advising us that as there was no scientific evidence to support the justification of a change in the law regarding commercial salmon fishing, it had been decided that no change was necessary or was to be made. We were told that this announcement was imminent and so we were beginning to breathe a sigh of relief as it appeared as if this problem was going to disappear. We were told that the various branches of the fisheries research division had been told to prepare all the evidence that the government could use to justify their decision that there was no necessity for this change in the law.

At this point however we were told that an important VIP visited a certain salmon data recording station on Deeside. There he spoke with a couple of young salmon scientists who were doing the data collecting and learned from them that there was not going to be a change in the law. We were also advised that some days later a leading government Scottish politician was invited to have lunch with this same VIP. Remarkably, with in days, we were told that the government had had a change of heart and they were now going to go ahead with the extension of the weekly closed time despite the lack of any supporting evidence. This decision to change the law was then lodged in the House of Commons library to give MPs the chance to pray against it. Sir Alec Buchannan Smith our local MP immediately prayed against it and several other Scottish MPs also recorded their opposition to this scientifically unsupported and unnecessary change in the law. This meant that there had to be a period of legally required consultation before a committee debate could be scheduled to take place in parliament. As I have explained earlier in this book the government's ruling party always has a built-in majority in any debate. The government could not get enough Scottish MPs to get this majority because Scottish government MPs knew that if they supported this bill they stood little chance of re-election. Therefore to make up the required numbers the government had placed two home counties, safe seat MPs on the committee. Sir Malcolm Forsythe, the then Scottish secretary, was to lead the debate for the government and he opened the debate and laid out their proposals. This was immediately ridiculed by Sir Alex along with other opposition MPs pointing out that there was no scientific support for this proposal. In addition it was morally wrong to remove the rights from one group of title holders which would immediately result in an increase in the value of property owned by a different set of individuals who all owned their fishing rights under the same legal title. Mr Forsythe and the government were comprehensively defeated in the debate. When the time limit for debate was reached and the division was held the government were successful and won the vote by one. Even then, one of the government English MPs recruited to make up the numbers stated that if he had been allowed to vote freely he would have voted against the government, but he apologised and said he had to follow the party line.

This was the beginning of the end for most salmon netting companies. We consulted about challenging the new laws in the courts and we were advised that if we fought it to the European court we would certainly win our case. We were further told that to get to take our case to Europe meant we had to exhaust the British legal system first. Unfortunately we were in addition advised that we could not take this as a group action. It had to be pursued as an individual action. If any action was pursued it was likely to take up to seven years to get to the European court and would undoubtedly cost more than fifty thousand pounds. None of us could possibly afford this sort of money so the b----rds had won.

Our landlords in Burghead bay then advised us that they were not prepared to continue our lease of the Burghead fishings after the end of the current season. They were to sell all their fishings to a charitable trust that had been set up to speed the removal of all netsmen. This was certainly the last straw. We had one year to go on our second ten year lease on the Hopeman fishings and we were obliged to notify the Crown Estate Commissioners who were our landlords that we would not be wishing to renew our lease once the current lease ran out. The situation at Portmahomack was even worse. You have to pay an annual fisheries assessment or rate to support the local river board. This value is set by local Government land assessors. We made an application to have our assessment reviewed because of the change of circumstances after the new law came into effect and also the reduced value of our fishery due to uncontrolled seal numbers which were making it unviable to operate. We had a hearing with the Rating Court but despite our expert witnesses and the obvious change in circumstances they refused us a reduction. If you own a salmon fishing title you are obliged to pay this annual fee. We pointed out that it was impossible to operate this fishery commercially and would have to close it down.

We were told we could sell our title or continue to pay this annual assessment of close on five thousand pounds in perpetuity as owners of this title. Their attitude was that salmon still passed along the coast whether we chose to try to catch them or not. There was absolutely no possibility of us being able to sell the title as we were recognised as very efficient operators and if we could not make it commercially viable nobody else would. Finally we had only two options, go bankrupt and forfeit the title or get the river board to accept the transfer of the title to them in release of the annual payment of rates. Fortunately they accepted this solution and we managed to sell our house and store in Portmahomack at a small profit which helped in a small way to offset the large capital loss on the purchase price of our fishing title made only a few years before.

We carried on operating the Hopeman fishery for the final year of our lease and at the end of this season we set about preparing and cataloguing all our assets for sale so that we could close down our salmon fishing company. All our assets were particularly specific to salmon netting and if we weren't able to make a commercial success of it there wasn't many people who thought they could. We had two large salmon cobbles, a tractor, a large numbers of heavy salmon net anchors and hundreds of yards of net moorings and floats. There were also ten of the large double headed bag nets all in good condition. Additionally there were fifty fathom long deep leaders for all the nets and much other auxiliary equipment including high pressure pumps for washing the nets and small motor pumps used in erecting the beach poles. It had taken us a lot of money and hard work to acquire all these supposed assets. The tax man had charged us fully for all these capital gains that we were supposed to have made, but now it was crunch time. I personally had £134,000 in written down capital assets invested in the company but after selling off everything and paying for the winding up of the company I received just over five and a half thousand pounds as my final settlement.

Thus ended my time in the fishing industries and I must stress I did not suffer alone. The Scots have long memories and it is therefore little wonder that the Conservatives have now few if any seats in Scotland. I had always voted conservative in my lifetime and was a close personal friend of Sir Alex Buchannan Smith and his wife and Sir Alex fought valiantly for our cause. I always believed that the party stood for small businesses and personal endeavour and risk-taking but I regret to say I was proved wrong. Unless there is a remarkable change in their policies and attitudes there is not a snowball's chance in hell that I would ever support them again.

I had to do something to support myself and my family for the final ten years before I reached retirement age. I had always been told that I was relatively gifted in art even winning the art prizes at school. I had for many years indulged in photography as my main hobby. In the years while employed in the salmon fishing I was at home for about five months in the year. During this time I had developed my skills and had reached a point where I did all my own developing, enlarging and printing of colour films both from slides and negatives. I had already done a few weddings and family commissions for friends and this gave me the confidence to lease premises and set myself up as a commercial photographer for the last ten years of my working life. I was fairly successful and even became internationally known and published as a glamour photographer but that must be another story.

Even several years after severing all my links with the fishing industries and the grey seal problems my reputed knowledge of grey seals came back to haunt me. I was summoned to appear as an expert witness for the defence of a salmon nets man who was accused of shooting seals other than in protection of his nets. The case was to be held in Wick sheriff court.

The prosecution's case was briefly that witnesses had seen the accused fisherman with his gun. They had then reported hearing shots at a specific time and then found bodies of seals on the beach. The beach in question was on the shore of the Pentlandfirth. The police had sent the seal carcases to the veterinary laboratories in Edinburgh for examination. They had discovered that the bullets that had killed the seals were of the same calibre as the weapon legally held by the fisherman. When I was finally called to give evidence I was first instructed to explain to the court why I was qualified to be called as an expert witness in this case. I explained to the court that I had been at every meeting held with the British Government on the seals issue for more than the last twenty years. I had also been recognised as a regular spokesperson in the media representing various groups associated with the interaction between grey seals and fish stocks, I had even been invited to go to Strasburg and address a major EEC fisheries committee on the subject. This was enough to convince the sheriff. I was told to start giving my evidence. I first said that the fact that the bullets that killed the seal were the same calibre as the accused's rifle meant nothing as probably in excess of eighty percent of all salmon netsmen used that same calibre of weapon when shooting seals. I then pointed out that at the time reported, on the day in question when the shots were heard, it was approaching low water. Yet the seal bodies were found at high water mark. If the seals found were supposed to have been shot at the time the shots were heard, they could only have got to high water mark if somebody had carried them there. I then turned to the biopsy reports which said that internally the seals had all suffered from severe decomposition and that the laboratory vets could not offer even a rough estimate of how long the seals had been dead. This was not consistent with the animals having been recently shot. I then turned to the photographic evidence the police had taken of the dead animals where they were found on the beach. The photographs all showed the seals to have massive distended bellies due to the compressed gas retained in their guts. I wet on to explain that grey seals have a natural negative buoyancy and that when they are shot in open water they sink slowly until they reach the sea bed. There they are carried along by the tide until such time as the gases developing in their guts expand enough to create a state of positive buoyancy to float them to the surface. I further went on to explain that the time taken to start a dead seal to float depended on water temperature and depth of water. I explained that in shallow water on sandy beaches where the water in summer was several degrees warmer and with low water pressure the body would begin to rise up in a matter of hours. However in areas like the Pentlandfirth with its exceptionally strong tides and deep water it could take several days before the developing gases in the stomach of the seal could reach the point that they could overcome the water pressure and start the carcase to float. Once this point was reached however with the reducing water pressure the body would shoot to the surface displaying the characteristic bloated body shape shown to us in the police photographs. Finally I turned to the location and asked if the court was aware that this particular beach was probably the only beach in British waters that had a tide that flowed in one direction for twenty two out of every twenty four hours. Therefore it was impossible for seals alleged to have been shot in that given location to possibly have found their way directly to the recorded position of the dead seals. There was total disbelief by the prosecution of my statement on tidal flows but I had brought along a current nautical almanac and a copy of the admiralty tidal charts of the Pentlandfirth to confirm my evidence. The prosecution then had a few more suppositions to make but they were easily overcome. The advocates then confirmed that the evidence was completed and the case complete. The sheriff then took a surprisingly short time to come to a decision. He mentioned the lack of specific ballistic evidence linking the accused gun to the shootings and that the prosecution had failed to point out that the evidence from the veterinary laboratory had pointed out the indeterminable estimated time of death of the seals. Finally he turned to my evidence and observed that in the light of what I can only describe as Mr McDonald,s almost encyclopaedic knowledge of his subject I declare the accused not guilty. Case dismissed. Perhaps my time studying grey seals had not been totally wasted after all.

Printed in Great Britain
by Amazon.co.uk, Ltd.,
Marston Gate.